Congratulations and love
to Cathy on her graduation
from University of Alberta
nursing School.
            Grandpa & Grandma Norton
Dec 11, 1987 Edmonton.

Favorite
Quotations
from the
Collection of
Thomas S. Monson

Favorite Quotations from the Collection of Thomas S. Monson

Deseret Book Company
Salt Lake City, Utah

Permissions have been granted for use of the following:

Six poems by Edgar Guest. Reprinted from *The Collected Verse of Edgar Guest* ©1934, used with permission of Contemporary Books, Inc., Chicago.

"If" by Rudyard Kipling. Excerpt from the poem "If" by Rudyard Kipling, copyright 1910 by Doubleday & Company, Inc. Reprinted from *Rudyard Kipling's Verse, Definitive Edition* by permission of The National Trust, The Macmillan Company of London and Basingstoke and Doubleday & Company, Inc.

Five songs from *Sing with Me*. Copyright ©1969 by Deseret Book Company. Used by permission.

Eight hymns from *Hymns*. Copyright ©1985 by Corporation of the President of The Church of Jesus Christ of Latter-day Saints. Used by permission.

"Bless This House" by Helen Taylor. From the song, music by May H. Brahe. Copyright 1927, 1932 by Boosey & Co., Ltd. Renewed 1954, 1959. Reprinted by permission of Boosey & Hawkes, Inc.

"Dad, I Love You" by F. Craig Sudbury. Permission granted by copyright holder, F. Craig Sudbury.

"Money" by Richard Armour. Reprinted from *An Armoury of Light Verse* by permission of Richard Armour, copyright holder.

"Storms Bring Out the Eagles" by Helen Steiner Rice. Reprinted with permission by Fleming H. Revell Company.

First printing October 1985

Library of Congress Cataloging-in-Publication Data
Main entry under title:

Favorite quotations from the collection of
Thomas S. Monson.

Includes index.
I. Quotations, English. I. Monson, Thomas S.,
1927–
PN6081.F36   1985   242'.809332   85-16279
ISBN 0-87747-749-3

Contents

v

Contents

Preface

◆

Over the years I have enjoyed collecting quotations, poems, and stories that might be used to illustrate important principles of the gospel. These are words of wisdom and inspiration that have influenced me with their simple but eloquent messages.

In this book you will find more than nine hundred of my favorite quotations and poems, the result of a lifetime of collecting. Efforts have been made to research the sources and to obtain permission, where needed, to publish the poems and quotations. For some of them, it has proved difficult, if not impossible, to find an original source or author. The publisher would welcome information from readers on these sources for subsequent printings of the book.

This book is not an official publication of The Church of Jesus Christ of Latter-day Saints. It has been prepared by me, and I alone am responsible for its contents.

May these short but important messages give you as much pleasure for your life as they have given me.

Special Thanks

I express my deep appreciation to Lynne F. Cannegieter for her assistance in the preparation of the manuscript; to E. Keith Eddington for his superb artistic talent in designing the volume; and to Ronald A. Millett, Eleanor Knowles, and Marci Chapman of Deseret Book Company for their meticulous efforts to identify the author of each quotation.

Home
and
Family

Home
and
Family

Some parents are fortunate and have their children born to them. Others, similarly blessed, have their children born for them.

Every boy, in his heart, would rather steal second base than an automobile.

Midwest City Bulletin

Building boys is better than mending men.

"And Jesus called a little child unto him, and set him in the midst of them, and said, Verily I say unto you, Except ye be converted, and become as little children, ye shall not enter into the kingdom of heaven. Whosoever therefore shall humble himself as this little child, the same is greatest in the kingdom of heaven."

Matthew 18:2-4

Once we thought that if we built enough playgrounds and other recreational facilities, juvenile delinquency would disappear. This turned out to be not so.

Robert F. Wagner

The most powerful combination of emotions in the world is not called out by any grand cosmic event, nor is it found in novels or history books; merely, it is found by a parent gazing down upon a sleeping child.

The baby that comes to your home is a sweet new blossom of humanity, fresh fallen from God's own home to flower on earth.

SHINE ON

My light is but a little one,
My light of faith and prayer;
But lo! it glows like God's great sun,
For it was lighted there.

Shine on, shine on,
Shine on bright and clear;
Shine on, shine on,
The day is here.

I may not hide my little light,
The Lord has told me so;
'Tis given me to keep in sight,
That all may see it glow.

Joseph Ballantyne

Home and Family

If you mothers will live your religion, then in the love and fear of God teach your children constantly and thoroughly in the way of life and salvation, training them up in the way they should go, when they are old they will not depart from it.

Brigham Young

"Train up a child in the way he should go: and when he is old, he will not depart from it."

Proverbs 22:6

The proper training of childhood is man's most sacred obligation. Children at birth are the most dependent and helpless of all creatures, yet they are the sweetest and the greatest of all things in the world. They come, or should come, from the Father pure and undefiled, their souls like stainless white paper on which is to be written the aspirations and achievements of a lifetime. Whether that scroll shall become the biography of a noble Christ-like life, or a series of blots and blurs depends largely, if not entirely, upon the guiding influence of parents, playmates and teachers.

David O. McKay

There are three fundamental things to which every child is entitled: first, a respected name; second, a sense of security; third, opportunities for development.

David O. McKay

◆

"Honour thy father and thy mother, as the Lord thy God hath commanded thee; that thy days may be prolonged, and that it may go well with thee, in the land which the Lord thy God giveth thee."

Deuteronomy 5:16

◆

Three influences in home life awaken reverence in children and contribute to its development in their souls. These are gentle guidance, courtesy by parents to each other and to children, and prayer in which children participate.

David O. McKay

◆

NIGHT BLESSING

Good night,
Sleep tight;
Wake up bright
In the morning light
To do what's right
With all your might.

◆

A recent survey of more than two thousand adolescents revealed some surprising things about today's kids. A majority of the kids believe in God and feel that more religion is needed in family life. The youngsters also expressed the wish that families could spend more time together as a family. The kids also said they wanted to communicate better with their parents.

◆

Home and Family

An independent nine-year-old boy announced to his mother and father at the breakfast table, "I am running away from home tomorrow. Who is going to drive me?"

What gift has Providence bestowed on man that is so dear to him as his children?

Marcus Tullius Cicero

STRANGE LANDS

Where do you come from, Mr. Jay?
"From the land of Play, from the land of Play."
And where can that be, Mr. Jay?
"Far away — far away."

Where do you come from, Mrs. Dove?
"From the land of Love, from the land of Love."
And how do you get there, Mrs. Dove?
"Look above — look above."

Where do you come from, Baby Miss?
"From the land of Bliss, from the land of Bliss."
And what is the way there, Baby Miss?
"Mother's kiss — Mother's kiss."

Laurence Alma Tadema

Next to eternal life, the most precious gift that our Father in Heaven can bestow upon man is his children.

David O. McKay

While in New Delhi, we received a telephone call saying there was a woman in a trash bin. When we arrived, we could hear her crying beneath the rubbish. She was covered with sores, her hair matted with filth. She continued to cry. She cried all the way to the home. She cried even after we had washed her and put her to bed. Finally she said, "I am not crying because I am dying. It's something else. It's because my son did it."

Curtis Pepper

Do your best to make certain you are the sort of person you want your children to become.

Of all lessons, the living lesson is the best. Children are surprisingly shrewd in detecting inconsistencies between the instructions and habits of their instructors. Besides, the teacher who seeks to live up to his own advice not only benefits his scholars, but his teachings exert a salutary influence upon himself, and he profits by his own lessons.

John Taylor

It is one of the greatest blessings that God ever bestowed upon children that they have had parents who were in possession of true principles in relation to their Heavenly Father, salvation, eternal life and were qualified and capable of teaching and traditioning their children in the same, that they may be qualified to fulfill the object of their creation.

Wilford Woodruff

Fatherhood is leadership — the most important kind of leadership. It has always been so; it always will be so. Father, with the assistance and counsel and encouragement of your eternal companion, you preside in the home. It is not a matter of whether you are the most worthy or best qualified, but it is a matter of law and appointment. You preside at the meal table, at family prayer. You preside at family home evening. And, as guided by the Spirit of the Lord, you see that your children are taught correct principles. It is your place to give direction relating to all of family life. You give fathers' blessings. You take an active part in establishing family rules and discipline. As a leader in your home, you plan and sacrifice to achieve the blessing of a unified and happy family. To do all of this requires that you live a family-centered life.

Spencer W. Kimball

We can make our houses homes and our homes heavens.

Spencer W. Kimball

At the age of ninety-two, Chauncey Depew was asked the question: "What is the most beautiful word in the English language?" He quickly replied: "Home."

Despite all new inventions and modern designs, fads, and fetishes, no one has yet invented, or will ever invent, a satisfying substitute for one's own family.

Stuart E. Rosenberg

I THINK WHEN I READ
THAT SWEET STORY OF OLD

I think when I read that sweet story of old,
When Jesus was here among men,
How he called little children like lambs to his fold,
I should like to have been with him then.

I wish that his hands had been placed on my head,
That his arms had been thrown around me,
That I might have seen his kind look when he said,
"Let the little ones come unto me."

Yet still to his footstool in prayer I may go,
And ask for a share in his love;
And if I thus earnestly seek him below,
I shall see him and hear him above.

Jemima Luke

A newborn child is almost the exact duplicate of an empty electronic computer, although superior to one in almost every way. What is placed in the child's brain during the first eight years of his life is probably there to stay. If you put misinformation into his brain during this period, it is extremely difficult to erase it. The most receptive age in human life is that of two or three years.

Glenn Doman

We say that children should be loyal to their parents. It is equally necessary that parents be loyal to their children.

Royal Bank of Canada Newsletter

We must spend more time with the children and less in clubs, bowling alleys, banquet and social gatherings. Fathers and mothers, we must come back home. We must sacrifice some of our other interests and organize our Church programs better so that both parents and youth will not be away from the home so much of the time. We must get more people to work in the Church so that the burden will not fall so heavily on the few. Then we must organize and do the maximum possible in the minimum amount of time, so that there can be more proper home life.

Spencer W. Kimball

A telephone survey was conducted to determine if parents knew where their children were at night. The telephone calls were made at 9:30 P.M. One interviewer was shocked when, on his first five calls, instead of the parents answering, the children answered — and they didn't know where their parents were!

I FOLLOW A FAMOUS FATHER

I follow a famous father,
His honor is mine to wear;
He gave me a name that was free from shame,
A name he was proud to bear.

I follow a famous father,
And him I must keep in mind;
Though his form is gone, I must carry on
The name that he left behind.

Edgar A. Guest

If we, as parents, will so order our lives that our children will know and realize in their hearts that we are in very deed Latter-day Saints, that we actually know what we are talking about, they, by seeking after the Lord, will get that same testimony.

Heber J. Grant

No matter what they may be without, are your homes pure within? Are morning prayers offered there regularly? Or do the things of this world take you away from your homes and make you deprive yourself of morning prayers with the children? Woe to that home where the mother abandons her holy mission or neglects the divine instruction, influence, and example — while she bows a devotee at the shrine of social pleasure; or neglects the essential duties in her own household, in her enthusiasm to promote public reform.

David O. McKay

Sign in front of a church in Sydney, Australia: Your home is the laboratory where your religion is tested.

The good parent says to his child, "You can become anything you want very much to become. My job is to help you become it." It's so important that we see our children as they really are. A true picture always has more lasting beauty.

Home and Family

The home is the basis of a righteous life, and no other instrumentality can take its place nor fulfill its essential functions. The utmost the auxiliaries can do is to aid the home in its problems, giving special aid and succor where such is necessary.

Harold B. Lee

There is no substitute for the home. Its foundation is as ancient as the world, and its mission has been ordained of God from the earliest times.

Joseph F. Smith

You hear it said that fathers want their sons to be what they feel they cannot themselves be, but I tell you it also works the other way. A boy wants something very special from his father.

Sherwood Anderson

Our children need our help — not our recriminations.

Sir John Hart

The greatest trust that can come to a man and woman is to have placed in their keeping the life of a little child.

David O. McKay

———————◆———————

We have been so anxious to give our children what we did not have that we have failed to give them what we should.

———————◆———————

I love these little people, and it is not a slight thing when they who are so fresh from God love us.

Charles Dickens

———————◆———————

Teaching is the noblest profession in the world. Upon the proper education of youth depend the permanency and purity of home and the safety and perpetuity of the nation. The parent gives the child an opportunity to live; the teacher enables the child to live well.

David O. McKay

———————◆———————

The Lord has given us a commandment that we shall teach our children the principles of the Gospel and have them baptized when they are eight years of age. If we fail to keep this commandment, the blessings that are promised to us by the Lord will be revoked, and we will have mourning and sorrow in seeing our children grow up without a desire to serve God. And in after years, when we endeavor to instill into their minds the principles of the Gospel, we will make a failure of it.

Heber J. Grant

———————◆———————

Your home is the most important school your child will ever attend, and you are his greatest teacher.

———————◆———————

Home and Family

Robert Frost said: "Home is the place where, when you get there, they have to let you in." To paraphrase Mr. Frost: "Home is the place where, when you get there, they *want* to take you in."

The most important work you will do within the Church will be within the walls of your own home.

Harold B. Lee

Marriage is the school of love.

Martin Luther

According to a study conducted by a professor at the University of Michigan, marriage is an aid to career advancement. Professor John E. Tropman surveyed six thousand men who were between the ages of forty-five and fifty-four. The men who were still married to their first wife had advanced the furthest, followed by those who had remarried. Men who were divorced, separated or widowed had advanced least.

Capsuled Comments

One generation of children, one entire generation of all the world of children, understood as they should be, loved as they ask to be, and so developed as they might be, would more than begin the millennium.

Francis Hodgson

Spoken of a mother who had been called from this mortal existence: "Mother is more than a memory; she is a living presence."

The most effectual way to establish the religion of Heaven is to live it.

Brigham Young

CHILDREN LEARN WHAT THEY LIVE

If a child lives with criticism, he learns to condemn.
If a child lives with hostility, he learns to fight.
If a child lives with fear, he learns to be apprehensive.
If a child lives with pity, he learns to feel sorry for himself.
If a child lives with jealousy, he learns to hate.
If a child lives with encouragement, he learns to be confident.
If a child lives with tolerance, he learns to be patient.
If a child lives with praise, he learns to be appreciative.
If a child lives with acceptance, he learns to love.
If a child lives with approval, he learns to like himself.
If a child lives with recognition, he learns to have a goal.
If a child lives with fairness, he learns justice.
If a child lives with security, he learns to have faith in himself and in those about him.
If a child lives with honesty, he learns what truth is.
And if a child lives with friendliness, he learns that the world is a nice place in which to live.

Dorothy L. Nolte

Home and Family

---◆---

In an essay on Quakers, an eight-year-old wrote: "Quakers are very meek, quiet people who never fight or answer back. My father is a Quaker, but my mother is not."

---◆---

Leaning on your family tree will never get you out of the woods.

---◆---

In a class in a Denver high school, the students were asked to prepare a letter to be written to a great man. Many of them addressed their letters to Mickey Mantle, President Kennedy, and others; but the daughter of President E.E. Drury of the Denver Stake wrote her letter to her father. In her letter she said: "I have decided to write this letter to you, Dad, because you are the greatest man that I have ever known. The overwhelming desire of my heart is that I might so live that I might have the privilege of sitting beside you and Mother and other members of the family in the celestial kingdom."

---◆---

Nothing is more beautiful than a mother who is proud of her husband and teaches her children to be like him.

Henry D. Moyle

---◆---

The greatest deterrent to juvenile delinquency would be for parents to show more love one for another.

Judge Phillip Gillian
Juvenile Court Judge

---◆---

Youth needs fewer critics and more models.

Today's children are caught in the whirlpool of status seeking. While fathers drive stately cars and mothers offer their homes to admiring inspection, they lose their sons and daughters. Children learn to judge by the symbols people display and not by people's individual worth.

There seems to be a power which the mother possesses in shaping the life of the child that is far superior, in my judgment, to the power of the father, and this almost without exception. . . . A mother's love seems to be the most perfect and the most sincere, the strongest of any love we know anything about.

Heber J. Grant

A worldwide survey of nearly one hundred thousand boys and girls resulted in the following list of do's and don'ts that every mother and father should memorize:
    1. Treat all your children with equal affection.
    2. Keep close to them.
    3. Make their friends welcome in your home.
    4. Don't quarrel in front of them.
    5. Be thoughtful to each other.
    6. Never lie to your children.
    7. Always answer their questions.
    8. Don't punish them in the presence of others.
    9. Be constant in affections and moods.
    10. Concentrate on good points — not failings.

Home and Family

Young people need rules to guide them and standards by which to judge themselves. The home takes its rightful and eminent place in preparing children for life when basic principles are quietly and firmly announced and lived up to. The final test is not how amenable young people are to compulsion of the law, but how far they can be trusted to obey self-imposed law.

Speaking to the 24th World Conference on Scouting held in Nairobi, Kenya, 17 July 1973, William C. Carter, president of Rotary International, said: "One of our chief challenges today in coping with youth and their world is the absence of the four restraining principles of earlier generations — namely: (1) fear of the Lord, (2) fear of parents, (3) fear of the schoolmaster, and (4) fear of the law."

Let the husband and father learn to bend his will to the will of his God, and then instruct his wife and children in this lesson of self-government by his example as well as by precept.

Brigham Young

If parents will continually set before their children examples worthy of their imitation and the approval of our Father in Heaven, they will turn the current and the tide of feelings of their children, and they, eventually, will desire righteousness more than evil.

Brigham Young

Home and Family

The motives of the twenty-four-year-old Lee Harvey Oswald, who pumped three shots into the young president from the sixth floor of a Dallas office building, are obscure; but they appear linked to a broken home, an indifferent mother, and an unsatisfactory marriage.

Warren Commission Report

Permanent homes in which sweet contentment abides are the strength of any nation. As contented individuals living in unselfish and loving communion make the happy homes, so contented, peaceful homes make the progressive, peaceful community; and groups of such communities constitute a peaceful, progressive nation. The perpetuity of our modern civilization depends upon well-ordered, well-governed homes.

David O. McKay

It is the duty of Latter-day Saints to teach their children the truth, to bring them up in the way they should go, to teach them the first principles of the Gospel, the necessity of baptism for the remission of sins and for membership in the Church of Christ; teaching them the necessity of receiving the gift of the Holy Ghost by the laying on of hands, which will lead them into all truth, and which will reveal to them things that have passed and things which are present with them, that they may comprehend the truth, and that they may walk in the light as Christ is in the light; that they may have fellowship with Him and that His blood may cleanse them from all sin.

Joseph F. Smith

Home and Family

The National Crime Commission, in its report to the President, declares that a major factor in the rapid rise in crime, particularly among persons under 21, is the failure of parents to train and discipline in the home.

What appears to be happening throughout the country, in the cities and in the suburbs, among the poor and among the well-to-do, is that parental, and especially paternal, authority over young people is becoming weaker.

The essential fact is that, according to the National Crime Commission, "America's best hope for reducing crime is to reduce juvenile delinquency and youth crime."

U.S. News and World Report

The mother has a greater influence over her posterity than any other person can have. And the question has arisen sometimes, "When does this education begin?" Our prophets have said, "When the spirit life from God enters into the tabernacle." The condition of the mother at the time will have its effect upon the fruit of her womb; and from the birth of the child, and all through life, the teachings and the example of the mother govern and control, in a great measure, that child, and her influence is felt by it through time and eternity.

Wilford Woodruff

Let the father and mother, who are members of this Church and Kingdom, take a righteous course and strive with all their might never to do a wrong, but to do good all their lives.

Brigham Young

Home and Family

◆

A visitor from out of town dropped into a home to visit the husband and wife of the house. After being met at the door by a small boy and being escorted to the living room, the young boy asked the visitor, "Are you related to us?"

The visitor replied, "Yes, I am a cousin on your father's side."

The boy replied, "In this house, Mister, you are on the wrong side!"

◆

LONDON (Reuters) — An American who wanted to trace his long-lost relatives in Britain has succeeded — for the price of one airmail letter to London.

Mike Archdale, 25, Miles City, Montana, knew only that his grandfather, Lionel Dawson Archdale, had emigrated to the United States from Northern Ireland at the end of the 19th Century. So Mike wrote to the only address he knew in London — the British Tourist Authority — and asked for help in finding his relatives.

The letter was opened at the tourist authority by a public relations officer — named Gilbert Archdale.

Gilbert Archdale did a little research and replied to Mike: "Hello. I'm your cousin!"

◆

The Sunday School teacher was describing how Lot's wife looked back and turned into a pillar of salt. Little Johnny was much interested. "My mother looked back once while she was driving," he explained, "and she turned into a telephone pole!"

◆

Home and Family

Daddy had a little boy;
His soul was white as snow.
He never went to Sunday School
'Cause Daddy didn't go.

He never heard the tales of Christ
That thrill a young child's mind;
While other children went to class
This child was left behind.

And so he grew from babe to youth;
Dad saw, to his dismay,
A soul that once was snowy white
Become a dingy grey.

Dad realized he'd soon be lost;
He tried to win him back
Before the soul that once was white
Became an ugly black.

So, not to lose his little boy,
(The fault be his, he knew),
He turned to God and humbly begged:
"Please tell me what to do."

Daddy had a little boy;
His soul was white as snow.
He never went to Sunday School,
'Cause Daddy didn't go.

There is too little religious devotion, love and fear of God
in the home; too much worldliness, selfishness,
indifference, and lack of reverence in the family.

Joseph F. Smith

He will call our sleeping dust to life, and they will still be joined together not only in spirit and body, but as happy parents they will come together again, standing at the head of their posterity as Adam and Eve will stand at the head of the multitude that are quickened and raised from the dead.

Charles W. Penrose

I pray you, my brethren and sisters, who have children in Zion, and upon whom rests the greater responsibility, teach them the principles of the Gospel, teach them to have faith in the Lord Jesus Christ and in baptism for the remission of sins when they shall reach the age of eight years. They must be taught in the principles of the Gospel of Jesus Christ by their parents, or the blood of the children will be upon the skirts of those parents.

Joseph F. Smith

Let us be worthy to be honored. Set your homes in order and have therein a spirit of joy with your companions, friends, and neighbors, that wherever you go the world will be brighter and happier because of your lives.

George A. Smith

Church activity should be led, not directed, by parents.

David O. McKay

Home and Family

Try today, and tomorrow, to make a change in your home by praying twice a day with your family. Call on your children and your wife to pray with you. Ask a blessing upon every meal you eat. Spend ten minutes in reading a chapter from the words of the Lord in the Bible, the Book of Mormon, the Doctrine and Covenants, before you retire, or before you go to your daily toil. Feed your spiritual selves at home, as well as in public places. Let love, and peace, and the Spirit of the Lord, kindness, charity, sacrifice for others, abound in your families. Banish harsh words, envyings, hatreds, evil speaking, obscene language, and innuendo, blasphemy, and let the Spirit of God take possession of your hearts. Teach to your children these things, in spirit and power, sustained and strengthened by personal practice. Let them see that you are earnest, and practice what you preach. Do not let your children out to specialists in these things, but teach them by your own precept and example, by your own fireside. Be a specialist yourself in the truth. Let our meetings, schools and organizations, instead of being our only or leading teachers, be supplements to our teachings and training in the home. Not one child in a hundred would go astray if the home environment, example and training were in harmony with the truth of the Gospel of Christ, as revealed and taught to the Latter-day Saints.

Joseph F. Smith

Do we want our homes to be happy? If we do, let them be the abiding place of prayer, thanksgiving, and gratitude.

George Albert Smith

THERE IS BEAUTY ALL AROUND

There is beauty all around
When there's love at home;
There is joy in every sound
When there's love at home.
Peace and plenty here abide,
Smiling sweet on every side.
Time doth softly, sweetly glide
When there's love at home.

In the cottage there is joy
When there's love at home;
Hate and envy ne'er annoy
When there's love at home.
Roses bloom beneath our feet;
All the earth's a garden sweet,
Making life a bliss complete
When there's love at home.

Kindly heaven smiles above
When there's love at home;
All the world is filled with love
When there's love at home.
Sweeter sings the brooklet by;
Brighter beams the azure sky;
Oh, there's one who smiles on high
When there's love at home.

John Hugh McNaughton

There can be no genuine happiness separate and apart from the home, and every effort made to sanctify and preserve its influence is uplifting to those who toil and sacrifice for its establishment.

Joseph F. Smith

Home and Family

I look upon the home as the basis from which radiate all good influences, and sometimes, I am sorry to say, bad influences which affect society. If, in every home in the United States, there were a competent mother and a helpful father, our officers of the law would have much less to do in protecting society from the lawless. In the art of home building, there should be manifest the work and skill of two artists—the father and the mother. If these two work at cross-purposes, the result of their efforts is frequently failure. If they work harmoniously, each supplying what the other needs as they daily work upon their living creations, the result will likely be boys and girls who will be a credit and an adornment—not a blight or a curse to humanity.

David O. McKay

LIKE MOTHER, LIKE SON

Do you know that your soul is of my soul such a part,
That you seem to be fibre and core of my heart?
None other can pain me as you, dear, can do,
None other can please me or praise me as you.

Remember the world will be quick with its blame
If shadow or stain ever darken your name.
"Like mother, like son" is a saying so true.
The world will judge largely the "mother" by you.

Be yours then the task, if task it shall be,
To force the proud world to do homage to me.
Be sure it will say, when its verdict you've won,
"She reaped as she sowed. Lo! this is her son."

Margaret Johnston Grafflin

———————◆———————

Sign which appears in the Relief Society room of the Olympus Stake Center located in Salt Lake City, Utah: Happiness is Homemade.

———————◆———————

WHAT I WANT MY CHILDREN TO REMEMBER ABOUT HOME

That their father and mother loved each other.

That our home was a happy one because we all worked to keep it so.

That each child was given every possible opportunity to develop his own personality.

That the books in the house were to be read if handled rightly, and there were no shelves under lock and key because of questionable contents.

That absolute truth abided there; no earnest questioner, however young, was put off with subterfuge or evasion.

That we believed in hospitality, in spite of any extra labor involved, and that our friends loved to come to visit us.

That Sunday was the happiest day of the week, and that we all looked forward to its coming because it was the day when we went to church together and then came home for an afternoon with Father in the midst.

That though Father and Mother worked hard and long at their respective jobs, they found time every day to keep informed on current events, to read good books, to think through to logical conclusions, and to pray.

———————◆———————

The weight of evidence points to early family life of the child as the primary factor leading to emotional disorders.

Dr. Rodnick, President
American Orthopsychiatric Association

———————◆———————

28

Home and Family

Reverence, as charity, begins at home.

David O. McKay

Next to loyalty as contributive to a happy home, I should like to urge continued courtship and apply this to grown people. Too many couples have come to the altar of marriage looking upon the marriage ceremony as the end of courtship instead of the beginning of an eternal courtship.

Let us not forget that during the burdens of home life — and they come — tender words of appreciation and courteous acts are even more appreciated than during those sweet days and months of courtship. It is after the ceremony and during the trials that daily arise in the home that a word of "thank-you," or "pardon me," or "if you please" on the part of the husband or wife contributes to that love which brought you to the altar.

It is well to keep in mind that love can be starved to death as literally as the body that receives no sustenance. Love feeds upon kindness and courtesy. It is significant that the first sentence of what is now known throughout the Christian world as the Psalm of Love is, "Love suffereth long, and is kind." The wedding ring gives no man the right to be cruel or inconsiderate.

David O. McKay

One of the questions after a study of magnets at Olympus Junior High located in Salt Lake City, Utah, was: What begins with *M* and picks things up? More than one-third of the students answered "Mother."

29

―――――――――――◆―――――――――――

DAD, I LOVE YOU

Dad, I love you, and do you know why?
Because of that special gleam in your eye
That tells me something important and true:
That I'm an important part of you.

I love you because I know there's no other
That you love more than the one I call mother.
I love you because you're always there,
Extending a hand to show that you care.

I love you because you're honest and strong;
You're courageous and steady when things go wrong.
I love you because in your steps I can trod.
Because I know you're a man of God.

Dad, I love you, and do you know why?
Because as a father you're quite a guy.
And because on earth you're what a father should be.
I know I'll be yours through eternity.

F. Craig Sudbury

―――――――――――◆―――――――――――

God has in reserve a time, or period appointed in His own
bosom, when He will bring all His subjects, who have
obeyed His voice and kept His commandments, into His
celestial rest. This rest is of such perfection and glory, that
man has need of a preparation before he can, according to
the laws of that kingdom, enter it and enjoy its blessings.
This being the fact, God has given certain laws to the
human family, which, if observed, are sufficient to prepare
them to inherit this rest.

Joseph Smith

―――――――――――◆―――――――――――

Home and Family

All that I am and all that I hope to be I owe to my angel mother. Blessings on her memory.

Abraham Lincoln

Keep religion in home life. We should make it obvious, both by our actions and our conversation, that we are seriously interested in religious things and believe in them ourselves: faith in God, in the divine mission of Jesus Christ, and in the restoration of the Gospel. Our religion should also take the form of honesty in our dealings with our family, our neighbors, and all with whom we come in contact. To give young people the right start in life, we must discuss with our children and friends questions of motive and subjects like birth, love, marriage, death, and destiny. Babson says, "One of the best things that could happen to America today would be a return to family prayers; the getting together after breakfast or in the evening for five or ten minutes for simple family worship! The saying of grace before meals would be a step in this direction." I am glad that that practice is general, I hope, throughout the Latter-day Saint homes.

David O. McKay

Endeavor to make your homes a little heaven, and try to cherish the good Spirit of God. Then let us as parents train up our children in the fear of God and teach them the laws of life. If you do, we will have peace in our bosoms, and peace in our families, and peace in our surroundings.

John Taylor

TELL ME THE STORIES OF JESUS

Tell me the stories of Jesus,
I love to hear;
Things I would ask him to tell me,
If he were here;
Scenes by the wayside,
Tales of the sea,
Stories of Jesus,
Tell them to me.

First let me hear how the children,
Stood round his knee;
And I shall fancy his blessing,
Resting on me;
Words full of kindness,
Deeds full of grace,
All in the lovelight
Of Jesus' face.

W. H. Parker

Let us all look at home and each one try to govern his own family and set his own house in order and do that which is required of us, realizing that each one is held responsible before the Lord for his or her individual actions only.

Wilford Woodruff

HOME, SWEET HOME

'Mid pleasures and palaces though we may roam,
Be it ever so humble, there's no place like home.

John Howard Payne

Home and Family

Woman was made of a rib out of the side of Adam; not out of his feet to be trampled upon by him, but out of his side to be equal with him, under his arm to be protected, and near his heart to be loved.

Matthew Henry

The primary responsibility and fundamentally so, is upon the parents to teach their children in light and truth. This commandment does not preclude or deny the Church the privilege of taking the children and aiding in their training. For this reason we have in the Church the auxiliary organizations, given by inspiration and commandment of the Lord.

Joseph F. Smith

AT SUNRISE

They pushed him straight against the wall;
The firing squad dropped in a row;
And why he stood on tiptoes,
Those men shall never know.

He wore a smile across his face
As he stood primly there,
The guns straight aiming at his heart,
The sun upon his hair;

For he remembered, in a flash,
Those days beyond recall,
When his proud mother took his height
Against the bedroom wall.

Rose Zagnoni Marinoni

Home and Family

◆

DEAREST CHILDREN, GOD IS NEAR YOU

Dearest children, God is near you
Watching o'er you day and night,
And delights to own and bless you,
If you strive to do what's right.
He will bless you, He will bless you,
If you put your trust in him.

Dearest children, holy angels
Watch your actions night and day;
And they keep a faithful record
Of the good and bad you say.
Cherish virtue! Cherish virtue!
God will bless the pure in heart.

Children, God delights to teach you
By His Holy Spirit's voice;
Quickly heed its holy promptings,
Day by day you'll then rejoice.
O prove faithful, O prove faithful
To your God and Zion's cause.

Charles L. Walker

◆

The holiest words my tongue can frame,
The noblest thoughts my soul can claim,
Unworthy are to praise the name
More precious than all others.
An infant, when her love first came,
A man, I find it still the same;
Reverently I breathe her name,
The blessed name of mother.

George Griffith Fether

◆

Home and Family

God could not be everywhere; therefore, he made mothers.

Jewish Proverb

I HAVE TWO LITTLE HANDS

I have two little hands folded snugly and tight,
They are tiny and weak yet they know what is right.
During all the long hours till daylight is through,
There is plenty in deed for my two hands to do.

Kind Father I thank thee for two little hands,
And ask thee to bless them till each understands
That children can only be happy all day,
When two little hands have learned how to obey.

Bertha A. Kleinmann

[A] great and important duty devolving upon this people is to teach their children, from their cradle until they become men and women, every principle of the Gospel, and endeavor, as far as it lies in the power of the parents, to instill into their hearts a love for God, the truth, virtue, honesty, honor and integrity to everything that is good. That is important for all men and women who stand at the head of a family in the household of faith. Teach your children the love of God; teach them to love the principles of the Gospel of Jesus Christ. Teach them to love their fellowmen, and especially to love their fellowship with the people of God. Teach them to honor the priesthood, to honor the authority that God has bestowed upon His Church for the proper government of His Church.

Joseph F. Smith

◆

A PARENT'S PRAYER

O God, make me a better parent. Help me to understand my children, to listen patiently to what they have to say and to answer all their questions kindly. Keep me from interrupting them, talking back to them, and contradicting them. Make me as courteous to them as I would have them be to me. Give me the courage to confess my sins against my children and to ask of them forgiveness when I know that I have done them wrong.

May I not vainly hurt the feelings of my children. Forbid that I should laugh at their mistakes or resort to shame and ridicule as punishment. Let me not tempt a child to lie and steal. So guide me hour by hour that I may demonstrate by all I say and do that honesty produces happiness.

Reduce, I pray, the meanness in me. May I cease to nag; and when I am out of sorts, help me, O Lord, to hold my tongue.

Blind me to the little errors of my children and help me to see the good things that they do. Give me a ready word for honest praise.

Help me to treat my children as those of their own age, but let me not exact of them the judgments and conventions of adults. Allow me not to rob them of the opportunity to wait upon themselves, to think, to choose, and to make decisions.

Forbid that I should ever punish them for my selfish satisfaction. May I grant them all of their wishes that are reasonable and have the courage always to withhold a privilege which I know will do them harm.

Make me so fair and just, so considerate and companionable

───────────── ◆ ─────────────

---

to my children, that they will have a genuine esteem for me. Fit me to be loved and imitated by my children.

With all Thy gifts, O God, do give me calm and poise and self-control.

Garry C. Myers

JESUS WANTS ME FOR A SUNBEAM

Jesus wants me for a sunbeam,
To shine for him each day;
In ev'ry way try to please him,
At home, at school, at play.

A sunbeam, a sunbeam,
Jesus wants me for a sunbeam;
A sunbeam, a sunbeam,
I'll be a sunbeam for him.

Jesus wants me to be loving,
And kind to all I see;
Showing how pleasant and happy
His little one can be.

I will ask Jesus to help me,
To keep my heart from sin;
Ever reflecting his goodness,
And always shine for him.

I'll be a sunbeam for Jesus,
I can, if I but try;
Serving him moment by moment,
Then live with him on high.

Nellie Talbot

THE CALL OF LOVE

Far above earth's tumult,
The call of love we hear,
Shall its gentle pleading
Fall on a heedless ear?

O hear the call of love,
O hear the call of love.
The call of love is to mercy
And pardon, and peace,
The call of love is to service
That never shall cease,
Till we shall enter
That land of promise
Where true joys abound,
Then onward press, my comrades,
We are gaining
We are gaining ground.

Not from far off country,
Or land across the sea,
Comes with earnest pleading
The call of love to me.

He who is my neighbor,
And needs a cheering word,
In his faintest whisper
That call of love is heard.

C. Austin Miles

Men are what their mothers made them.

Ralph Waldo Emerson

Home and Family

BLESS THIS HOUSE

Bless this house, O Lord we pray,
Make it safe by night and day;
Bless these walls, so firm and stout,
Keeping want and trouble out;
Bless the roof and chimneys tall,
Let Thy peace lie over all;
Bless this door, that it may prove
Ever open to joy and love.

Bless these windows shining bright,
Letting in God's heavenly light;
Bless the hearth a-blazing there,
With smoke ascending like a prayer;
Bless the folk who dwell within,
Keep them pure and free from sin;
Bless us all that we may be
Fit, O Lord, to dwell with Thee,
Bless us all that one day we
May dwell, O Lord, with Thee.

Helen Taylor

I believe the most valuable thing a mother can teach her
child is belief, confidence, and faith in a loving God — to
reach outward and upward beyond himself for strength
and courage — and to instill in that child the simple faith
that he or she is a child of God with a purposeful life ahead.
Life is filled with the unexpected: accidents, deaths,
hazards, fears. Mother, father, the light switch, water in
the tap may not always be there. But resource to God is
always available.

G. Homer Durham

Proclaiming
the
Gospel

Proclaiming
the
Gospel

---◆---

EXCERPT FROM THE WENTWORTH LETTER

Our missionaries are going forth in different nations. The standard of truth has been erected; no unhallowed hand can stop the work from progressing. Persecutions may rage, mobs may combine, armies may assemble, calumny may defame; but the truth of God will go forth boldly, nobly and independent, till it has penetrated every continent, visited every clime, swept every country and sounded in every ear, till the purposes of God shall be accomplished, and the Great Jehovah shall say the work is done.

Joseph Smith

---◆---

Go in all meekness and sobriety, and preach Jesus Christ and Him crucified; not to contend with others on account of their faith, or systems of religion, but pursue a steady course. This I deliver by way of commandment, and all who observe it not will pull down persecution upon their heads, while those who do shall always be filled with the Holy Ghost; this I pronounce as a prophecy.

Joseph Smith

---◆---

"Wherefore, now let every man learn his duty, and to act in the office in which he is appointed, in all diligence. . . ."

Let the idea be emphasized throughout the entire church . . . that when a young man enlists under the missionary banner it means that he is superior in every way: in character, in faith, and in a desire to serve the Lord.

True Christianity is love in action. There is no better way to manifest love for God than to show an unselfish love for one's fellowmen. That is the spirit of missionary work.

God bless the missionaries wherever they are today, for they are God's servants, as long as they keep themselves pure and spotless from the sins of the world. I testify to you that His Spirit is guiding them, magnifying them in their youth and making them a power in preaching the Gospel of Jesus Christ.

David O. McKay

The kind of men we want as bearers of this Gospel message are men who have faith in God; men who have faith in their religion; men who honor their priesthood; men in whom the people who know them have faith and in whom God has confidence — and not some poor unfortunate beings who are wanting to leave a place because they cannot live in it. We want men full of the Holy Ghost and the power of God, that they may go forth weeping, bearing precious seed and sowing the seeds of eternal life, and then returning with gladness, bringing their sheaves with them. Men who bear the words of life among the nations ought to be men of honor, integrity, virtue and purity; and this being the command of God to us, we shall try to carry it out.

John Taylor

The tabulated results of questions asked three thousand recent converts:

1. How did you first hear the gospel?
   Missionary 45%
   Neighbor 15%
   Kin 40%

2. What phase of the gospel attracted you to it?
   Teachings about God 35%
   The Book of Mormon 26%
   The Plan of Salvation 39%

3. If missionaries first brought the gospel, what impressed you most about them?
   Their apparent conviction 70%
   Their knowledge of the Bible 30%

4. Which do you feel helped you most to conversion?
   Cottage meetings 25%
   Branch meetings with Saints 10%
   Personal talks with missionaries and
      others 65%

5. When did you sense that the restored gospel was true?
   Right at first 65%
   After all the lessons 35%

I feel like shouting hallelujah, all the time, when I think that I ever knew Joseph Smith, the Prophet.

Brigham Young

Conversion occurs when we see with our eyes, hear with our ears, and understand with our hearts.

"I will go and do the things which the Lord hath commanded, for I know that the Lord giveth no commandments unto the children of men, save he shall prepare a way for them that they may accomplish the thing which he commandeth them."

1 Nephi 3:7

"And if it so be that you should labor all your days in crying repentance unto this people, and bring, save it be one soul unto me, how great shall be your joy with him in the kingdom of my Father!

"And now, if your joy will be great with one soul that you have brought unto me into the kingdom of my Father, how great will be your joy if you should bring many souls unto me!"

D&C 18:15-16

"And ye shall go forth in the power of my Spirit, preaching my gospel, two by two, in my name, lifting up your voices as with the sound of a trump, declaring my word like unto angels of God."

D&C 42:6

There never was a set of men, since God made the world, under a stronger responsibility to warn this generation. We are required to do this. This is our calling. It is our duty. It is our business.

Wilford Woodruff

Proclaiming the Gospel

◆

If I could have my wish today, it would be that every one of God's children could hear this glorious message and earnestly give consideration to it. I am sure that thereby there would come into countless hearts through the whisperings of the Spirit that joy and happiness which attend our own testimonies of the truth. Through our missionary system we have made a tremendous contribution to this end, but it is not enough. We must find new ways to inform and persuade the world, and if we are faithful and truly devoted, God will open the way. That is my conviction.

I know as I know that I live that this is His kingdom. He will never desert it. God help all of us never to desert Him

Stephen L Richards

◆

"I will go before your face. I will be on your right hand and on your left, and my Spirit shall be in your hearts, and mine angels round about you, to bear you up."

D&C 84:88

◆

There is nothing we can't do in the building of the Lord's kingdom if we have the desire, do the work, and have the faith.

Henry D. Moyle

◆

Missionary work is the lifeblood of the Kingdom. When the blood stops flowing, the Kingdom stops growing.

Spencer W. Kimball

◆

◆

"Behold I have given unto you my gospel, and this is the gospel which I have given unto you — that I came into the world to do the will of my Father, because my father sent me.

"And my Father sent me that I might be lifted up upon the cross; and after that I had been lifted up upon the cross, that I might draw all men unto me, that as I have been lifted up by men even so should men be lifted up by the Father, to stand before me, to be judged of their works, whether they be good or whether they be evil."

3 Nephi 27:13–14

◆

"I know that which the Lord hath commanded me, and I glory in it. I do not glory of myself, but I glory in that which the Lord hath commanded me; yea, and this is my glory, that perhaps I may be an instrument in the hands of God to bring some soul to repentance; and this is my joy."

Alma 29:9

◆

Our missionaries are not salesmen, with wares to peddle; rather, they are servants of the Most High God, with a testimony to bear, truth to teach, and souls to save.

Thomas S. Monson

◆

What a thrilling thing it is to see an aggressive, resourceful, willing, untiring, well-directed, spiritual missionary who can do the right things on his own initiative and keep on doing them to the end.

◆

Proclaiming the Gospel

If you go on a mission to preach the Gospel with lightness and frivolity in your hearts, looking for this and that, and to learn what is in the world, and not having your minds riveted—yes, I may say riveted—on the cross of Christ, you will go and return in vain. Go forth weeping, bearing precious seed, full of the power of God, and full of faith to heal the sick even by the touch of your hand, rebuking and casting out foul spirits, and causing the poor among men to rejoice, and you will return bringing your sheaves with you. Let your minds be centered on your missions and labor earnestly to bring souls to Christ.

Brigham Young

The ABCs of missionary work:
> A = Attitude
> B = Behavior
> C = Companion

Missionaries of the present-day ministry must *believe* the Gospel; they must *preach* the Gospel; but especially, they must *live* the Gospel.

Christian Beacon

"I am not ashamed of the Gospel of Christ: for it is the power of God unto salvation." (Romans 1:16.) If we are not ashamed of the Gospel, we should not be ashamed to teach it; and if we are not ashamed to teach it, we should not be ashamed to live it.

Delbert L. Stapley

49

It is by no means improbable that some future textbook, for the use of generations yet unborn, will contain a question something like this: "What historical American of the nineteenth century has exerted the most powerful influence upon the destinies of his countrymen?" And it is by no means impossible that the answer to that interrogatory may thus be written: "Joseph Smith, the Mormon Prophet." And the reply, absurd as it doubtless seems to most men now living, may be an obvious commonplace to their descendants. The man who established a religion in this age of free debate, who was and is today accepted by thousands as a direct emissary from the Most High—such a rare human being is not to be disposed of by pelting his memory with unsavory epithets.

Josiah Quincy, Jr.

"For though I preach the gospel, I have nothing to glory of: for necessity is laid upon me; yea, woe is unto me, if I preach not the gospel!"

1 Corinthians 9:16

You are called upon to declare the words of eternal life with vigor, humility, and faith—bringing out of darkness those who sit in darkness.

Joseph Fielding Smith

———————————◆———————————

Presidents, the testimony of a mission president to a wavering missionary is the most important message he could convey.

Harold B. Lee

———————————◆———————————

Your mission is preparation. It is your school for eternity. You won't forget that, will you? This mission is not just a two-year stretch. This is the time when you cultivate the seeds of godhood so that you can help other people on their way toward exaltation. How small are we who think of the mission as just being a stretch of time, some physical things to do, a little studying to do, some praying. This is the most purposeful thing, perhaps, you have ever done in your life and possibly the most purposeful thing that some of you will ever do. It's up to you to let this be the prelude to your life, to let it be the beginning of a great and glorious life.

Spencer W. Kimball

———————————◆———————————

FOUR GIFTS FOR CONVERTS

1. Give them an understanding to live by.
2. Give them someone to walk with.
3. Give them something to do.
4. Give them something to feed on.

Gordon B. Hinckley

———————————◆———————————

51

Proclaiming the Gospel

◆

There are many excellent men but very few really good missionaries. A good missionary is a man who has sociability, whose friendship is permanent and sparkling, who can ingratiate himself into the confidence and favor of men who are in darkness.

Joseph F. Smith

◆

Dear Mom and Dad:

I want to thank you from the bottom of my heart for the many wonderful things you have done for me.

I want to thank you for listening to the wonderful message the elders presented to you when they knocked at your door. I thank you for the way you grasped the gospel and made it the mold around which you shaped your lives and the lives of your children.

I love both of you very much. Thank you for the way in which you taught me, for your love which you expressed in many ways. Thank you for directing me in the right paths — for showing me instead of forcing me.

I am thankful for your beautiful testimonies and for the guiding love in which you helped me gain mine. I know the gospel is true. My few experiences out here have strengthened my testimony. I pray that I can live up to your expectations. . . . I should, with the Lord's help.

Thank you again, Mom and Dad.

> Your loving son,
> David

◆

Helps
for
Leadership

Helps
for
Leadership

Let each bishop attend faithfully to his ward and see that every man and woman is well and faithfully and profitably employed; that the sick and aged are properly cared for, that none suffer.

Let each bishop be a tender and indulgent father to his ward, administering a word of comfort and encouragement here, a word of advice and counsel there, and a word of chastisement in another place, where needed, without partiality, wisely judging between man and man, caring for and seeking earnestly the welfare of all, watching over the flock of God with the eye of a true shepherd, that wolves and dogs may not enter among the flock and rend them.

Brigham Young

The best way to help a man increase his output, or his leadership of any kind, is to help build the man. Help him increase his stature as a man, and he will just naturally do better — on the job and off.

Earl Nightingale

◆

Are those for whom you are responsible in a "Never, Never Land?" Never the object of concern, never the recipient of needed aid?

Thomas S. Monson

◆

Most church workers are like a clock:
1. Some run too fast.
2. Some run too slow.
3. Some run too quietly.
4. Some run too noisily.

Church workers, like clocks, need to be regulated. This is the responsibility of the executives.

◆

One hundred years from now, it will not matter what kind of car I drove, what kind of house I lived in, how much I had in my back account, nor what my clothes looked like. But the world may be a little better because I was important in the life of a boy.

◆

Big-minded executives do not feel called upon to defend their position, regardless of whether it is right or wrong. A quite moderate degree of conciliatory behavior will probably win a good measure of what is desired.

◆

There is nothing noble in feeling superior to some other person. The true nobility is in being superior to your previous self.

Hindu Proverb

◆

56

Helps for Leadership

———————◆———————

There can be no substitute for integrity in a person seeking to be a leader. This involves more than simple abstention from crime. It includes adherence to ethical principles and soundness of moral character. Fairness and impartiality are especially needed in the character of a person in authority. He must speak the truth to those under him and keep his promises to everyone, regardless of status.

———————◆———————

A person in authority is not necessarily a saint, an artist, a philosopher, or a hero; but he respects truth, appreciates what is beautiful, knows how to behave himself, and is courageous in meeting his obligations. He will have intellectual curiosity and will be always learning. He is tolerant, liberal, and unshockable. If he is not always affable and urbane, he at least is never truculent or overbearing. He will be a cultured, broad-minded scholar who lives according to the spirit of reasonableness.

———————◆———————

The true function of leadership is to bring out the best efforts of others, and people most willingly pay heed to those whom they consider most able to direct.

———————◆———————

HOW TO CHOOSE LEADERS

1. Determine requirements of office.
2. Evaluate capacity.
3. Evaluate attitude.
4. Consider past performance.
5. Use inspiration.
6. Seek counsel.

———————◆———————

◆

CHECKLIST FOR EXECUTIVES

1. Do you know and call each of your officers and teachers by name?
2. Do you know something about the home life and background of all your officers and teachers?
3. Do you associate in an informal way with all your officers and teachers outside of the Church organization with which you are affiliated?
4. Do you show by your speech and by your actions that you are loyal to the ward bishopric, stake presidency and other Church authorities?
5. Are you loyal to those who are working under your direction?
6. Do you consider the suggestions and the needs and desires of others in your organization before making important decisions?
7. Do you show the officers and teachers in your organization by your words and your actions that you personally appreciate their efforts?
8. Do you give instructions and suggestions in the same considerate way you would like to receive instructions from others?
9. Do you occasionally review the goals and objectives of your organization with your officers and teachers?
10. Do you assist your teachers in finding transportation to meetings?
11. Do you stress the importance of prayer in the fulfilling of assignments?
12. Do you set an example of which you can be proud in Church activities both inside and outside your own organization?
13. Are you happy in your assignment and helping to make your coworkers happy too?
14. Are you striving to improve your effectiveness as an

◆

◆

executive from day to day and from week to week?

15. Are you completely satisfied with the results of your work, or are you conscious of the fact that improvements can be made?

16. Are you continually wanting to resign, or do you feel that you have a responsibility which you should discharge until those in authority release you?

17. Are the purposes of our Father in Heaven uppermost in your mind as you carry out your responsibilities?

◆

Promise without performance is an adult hypocrisy.

◆

Followship comes before leadership.

◆

If you must be aggressive, use tact. If you are right and others are wrong, use delicacy in telling them.

Royal Bank of Canada Newsletter

◆

The manager must, as one executive put it, learn how to disturb the equilibrium without upsetting the apple cart. Seek help, accept help, and give help generously.

Royal Bank of Canada Newsletter

◆

The good administrator is tolerant of other people's ideas and is not dogmatic about his own. He keeps in mind the necessity of yielding to everyone his rights.

◆

Helps for Leadership

---◆---

A good leader inspires other men with confidence in him; a great leader inspires them with confidence in themselves.

---◆---

Two basic qualities of delegation are the superior's authority to delegate and his own, as well as his subordinate's, responsibility for the final results. A third important factor is accountability. An employee's accountability is his responsibility to keep the boss informed as to how the delegated task is progressing. This responsibility can be encouraged or discouraged by the manager's reaction to the employee's reports. If the boss continually finds fault with mistakes instead of trying to help correct them, the employee will feel like a failure and will no longer care about doing his best on the task at hand.

Capsuled Comments

---◆---

The real art of management is understanding men — not just as statistics, or as parts of a large whole, but as individuals. What, for example, makes one man suspicious and distant and another man outgoing and happy? The same stimulus might call forth both reactions. It is up to the manager to know what makes people tick, to recognize talent and to see one person's strength and another person's weakness.

While man has found reason, logic, and order in a number of the phenomena that surround him, he himself remains a puzzle of great potential. Isn't he worth knowing? As A. M. Sullivan put it, "*Man* is still the most engaging syllable in management."

Capsuled Comments

---◆---

Helps for Leadership

A good leader takes the position that the other fellow is capable of being far more than he is, and it is the leader's responsibility to help him develop to his fullest potential.

Lawrence A. Appley

Good leadership consists of showing average people how to do the work of superior people.

John D. Rockefeller

Nobody is especially interested in how hard a manager has worked, but in what he has produced.

Royal Bank of Canada Newsletter

Wide general acquaintance with the humanities may not give a man the technical qualifications to put across a big deal, but it will prepare him to grasp the essentials of the human situation; and all deals, big or little, resolve themselves into dealing with human beings.

Royal Bank of Canada Newsletter

When performance is measured, performance improves. When performance is measured and reported back, the rate of improvement accelerates.

Thomas S. Monson

'Twas a sheep, not a lamb, that strayed away
In a parable Jesus told;
A grown-up sheep had gone astray
From the ninety and nine in the fold.

Out on the hillside, out in the cold,
'Twas a sheep the Good Shepherd sought.
And why for the sheep should we earnestly long
And so earnestly hope and pray?

Because there is danger, if they go wrong;
They will lead the lambs astray.
For the lamb will follow the sheep, you know,
Wherever the sheep may stray.
When the sheep go wrong it will not be long
'Til the lambs are as wrong as they.

And so, with the sheep, we earnestly plead
For the sake of the lambs today;
If the lambs are lost, what a terrible cost
Some sheep will have to pay.

Of the best rulers,
The people (only) know that they exist;
The next best they love and praise;
The next they fear;
And the next they revile.

When they do not command the people's faith,
Some will lose faith in them,
And then they resort to oaths!
But (of the best) when their task is accomplished,
    their work done
The people all remark, "We have done it ourselves."

Laotse

62

Helps for Leadership

In the interior of our consciousness each of us has a sort of private Hall of Fame, reserved exclusively for the real leaders who have influenced the direction of our lives. Relatively few of the many men who have exercised authority over us from childhood through adult life meet our test for admission to this precinct. That test has very little to do with the outward trappings of power or an abundance of this world's goods. The leaders whom we admit into this private sanctuary of our reflective meditation are usually those who set our hearts afire with devotion to truth, who made obedience to duty seem the essence of manhood, who transformed some ordinary routine occurrence so that it became a vista whence we saw the man we aspired to be. The leaders of our choosing were men who personified faith and fidelity, who were instinctively repulsed by what was unclean or unfair, in whose presence evil cringed and seemed repulsive — men who were blessed with a faculty for striking a direct blow at the painted face of falsehood and deceit and were capable of awakening in us a desire to develop to the fullest our own talents and aptitudes.

Edward Hanify

A leader must be more than an administrator. He must have executive abilities, true, but he must know how to vitalize the power of people. He must understand how to build enthusiasm and self-reliance in those he directs by setting a good example himself. In influencing others to strive willingly for mutual objectives, the leader must radiate confidence and create an instant image of competence. This can be more powerful than any other quality.

Lou Laurel

Helps for Leadership

A good formula for successful leadership is:
1. Communicate
2. Motivate
3. Meditate
4. Generate

The man whose authority is recent is always stern.

Aeschylus

When in charge — ponder.
When in trouble — delegate.
When in doubt — mumble, then refer the problem to a
coordinating committee for review.

If you are one of those managers who just can't seem to
communicate with people in meetings, chances are that
there is a good reason for your problem. It helps if your
presentations are carefully planned and organized, and this
includes full explanations of any terms or abbreviations
that might be difficult for your colleagues to understand.
Another point to remember is that too much detail can kill
a presentation. Other features of a successful presentation
include a definitely stated goal, good use of audiovisual
aids, good delivery, plenty of proofs and examples, and
able handling of questions.

If you want to give a light to others, you have to glow
yourself.

Helps for Leadership

People may talk and never teach, unless they practice what they preach.

I think that to have known one good man . . . helps our faith in God, in ourselves, and in each other more than many sermons.

George William Curtis

The eye's a better student and more willing than the ear.
Fine counsel is confusing, but example's always clear,
And the best of all the preachers are the men who live their
    creeds,
For to see the good in action is what everybody needs.

I can soon learn how you do it if you'll let me see it done.
I can watch your hands in action, but your tongue too fast
    may run;
And the lectures you deliver may be very wise and true,
But I'd rather get my lesson by observing what you do.

For I may not understand you and the high advice you give;
But there's no misunderstanding how you act and how
    you live.

Edgar A. Guest

If we want knowledge without values, we can find it in almanacs. If we want information without motivation, we can get it in computers. But if we are looking for leadership, then the first test is for character.

Norman Cousins

Helps for Leadership

A good example has twice the value of good advice.

Don't be an average leader, for an average leader is only the worst of the best and the best of the worst.

HOW TO DISCOVER SOLUTIONS TO PROBLEMS

1. Recognize your problem.
2. Ask: Where could we improve?
3. Concentrate on the problems one at a time.
4. Talk through the problem with others.
5. Pray and fast.
6. Gather all available material at hand.
7. List and discuss possibilities leading to a solution.
8. Trust the inspiration which will come.
9. Put solutions into immediate operation.

TEN COMMANDMENTS FOR SALESMEN

1. Be agreeable.
2. Know your business.
3. Tell the truth.
4. Don't argue.
5. Make it plain.
6. Be dependable.
7. Remember names and faces.
8. Beware of egotism.
9. Think success.
10. Be human.

Dr. Frank Crane

MY CHUM

He stood at the crossroads all alone,
The sunlight in his face.
He had no thought for the world unknown —
He was set for a manly race.
But the roads stretched east and the roads stretched west,
And the lad knew not which road was best,
So he chose the road that led him down,
And he lost the race and the victor's crown.
He was caught at last in an angry snare
Because no one stood at the crossroads there
To show him the better road.

Another day at the self-same place,
A boy with high hopes stood.
He, too, was set for a manly race;
He, too, was seeking the things that were good.
But one was there who the roads did know.
And that one showed him which way to go.
So he turned from the road that would lead him down,
And he won the race and the victor's crown.
He walks today the highway fair
Because one stood at the crossroads there
To show him the better way.

Unknown

The job of the executive is to think, plan, direct, check, and inspire.

Formula for failure: Try to please everybody.

---◆---

A real leader has the ability to get others to work willingly through his influence and example. His efforts are directed toward influencing people to want to do certain things — not to make them obey commands.

---◆---

Six qualities great leaders possess:

1. Knowledge
2. Imagination
3. Solid thinking
4. Initiative
5. Hard work
6. Knowledge of the relationship between God and man

David O. McKay

---◆---

The manager is expected to originate, visualize, organize, energize, and supervise.

Royal Bank of Canada Newsletter

---◆---

ATTRIBUTES OF A GOOD LEADER

1. A sense of purpose and direction
2. Decisiveness
3. Physical and nervous energy
4. Integrity, loyalty
5. Technical mastery
6. Friendliness and affection
7. Faith
8. Endurance
9. Teaching skills

---◆---

THE MANLY LEADER

He readies each assignment
With vigor and with vim;
He gets it clearly in his head
Until it's part of him.
When he gives a lesson,
His eyes know where to look.
They like to meet a young man's eyes —
Not pages of a book.
The conscientious leader
Is much concerned for youth.
His lips and tongue and vocal cords
Will always speak the truth.
Because he is a gentleman,
His knees you seldom see,
But you can tell he has them
For he's on them frequently.
His legs may not be muscle greats;
They're fit, though, for the climb.
And one thing's sure: they'll get him there,
Every time — on time.
In the reach for something better
It is just as you suppose:
This super he-man leader
Is always on his toes!

The manager's chief need, given technical skill to handle the mechanics of his particular business, is to understand people. Some are born with this quality; others acquire it. The manager must have it either by inheritance or by study and practice.

Royal Bank of Canada Newsletter

◆

We teach best by example. Edmund Burke said, "Example is the school of mankind, and they will learn at no other." To me one of the clearest examples of teachers who care about the people they teach comes out of the music classroom. Here are musicians, performers themselves, some sufficiently talented to be recitalists. Yet they sit in a room with a beginning violinist, listening to the squawk and screech and scrape of the bow across those strings. How can they stand it—the violation of their art, this desecration of music? Because the music teacher cares more about that child than about the art itself.

Someone has said, "A mediocre teacher tells, a good teacher explains, a superior teacher demonstrates; but the great teacher inspires." I'm a teacher and a writer today because I was inspired by a high school teacher of English in London, Ontario—a man named David Carr. His love for books and ideas was exceeded only by his love for people. He was the first person to bring literature to life for me, the first to encourage me to write for publication in the city newspaper. "A teacher affects eternity," said Henry Adams. "He can never tell where his influence stops."

D. Bruce Lockerbie

◆

A good executive in any field, including the spiritual, increases the output of all those with whom he works.

◆

A successful general is one under whose leadership the staff, as well as the rank and file, will work and die with enthusiasm.

Walter Gifford

◆

Helps for Leadership

In all our leadership it is well for us to remember that each of us is a partner of our Heavenly Father in helping to lift the individual toward eternal life. Nowhere does this come to us more forcibly than from the meeting on the mount of Moses with the Lord. The Lord there showed Moses the earth below, "and there was not a particle of it which he did not behold." (Moses 1:27.)

Man attains in the measure that he aspires.

James Allen

There is no greater responsibility in the world than the training of a human soul.

One of the marks of executive leadership is the capacity to assign responsibility, give authority, and hold men responsible for that authority. And, of course, he must see to it that the job gets done.

Five aspects in appointing and supervising successful leaders:

1. Proper selection.
2. Dignified call (no ditch-bank type).
3. Proper vision (let them know what is expected).
4. Set them on fire.
5. Follow up.

Spencer W. Kimball

I believe that a business's greatest assets are its human assets, and that the improvement of their value is both a matter of material advantage and moral obligation. I believe that employees must be treated as honorable individuals, justly rewarded, encouraged in their progress, fully informed and properly assigned and that their lives and work must be given meaning and dignity on and off the job. If I have the supervision of so much as one other person, I will strive to honor these principles in practice.

Clarence Francis

Successful sales executives know when and how to delegate responsibility and authority. The answers to the following questions can determine your ability to delegate:

1. Do you take work home?
2. Are your work hours longer than your subordinates'?
3. When you are off for a day does your "in" basket fill up?
4. Are you still doing jobs you handled before your last promotion?
5. Are you constantly interrupted by questions?
6. Do you work on details others could handle?
7. Do you like to keep tabs on everything?
8. Is there always a deadline to meet?

If "yes" is your answer to five or more of the above inquiries, then you need to learn more about the art of delegating.

Father to leader: "I wish you would do something for my boy."
Leader to father: "I wish you would, too."

One of the qualities of leadership which contributes most to success is seldom listed. This trait is often overlooked or unobserved because other factors stand out. It may be the reason for the drive or even the ambition. Certainly it contributes to the awareness and the constant emphasis on performance.

A leader constantly seeks ways to do better whatever needs to be done. If a person with this quality will continue positive application of this negative factor, that person will have a leadership role.

The quality: dissatisfaction. To make the unsatisfactory satisfactory or better is the mark of leadership. Never be satisfied with less than top performance, and progress will be the reward.

Vince Lombardi

The world's most unrewarding activity is to "follow the follower." It cannot supplant "follow the leader."

MAN-MAKING

We are blind until we see
That in the human plan
Nothing is worth the making if
It does not make the man.

Why build these cities glorious
If man unbuilded goes?
In vain we build the world, unless
The builder also grows.

Edwin Markham

The calling of the gospel teacher is one of the noblest in the world. The good teacher can make all the difference in inspiring boys and girls and men and women to change their lives and fulfill their highest destiny. The importance of the teacher has been beautifully described by Daniel Webster when he said, "If we work upon marble, it will perish; if we work upon brass, time will efface it; but if we work upon immortal minds, if we imbue them with principles and the just fear of God and love of our fellowman, we engrave upon those tablets something that will brighten through all eternity."

With this philosophy in mind, the Church has established a program for teacher development. Teachers in the Church must be prepared to meet the challenge to those forces that seek to mold the minds of men. Satan is on the move as never before. The world is changing rapidly in both positive and negative ways. This program is prepared for three groups: present teachers, prospective teachers, and Church leaders. And, of course, the aim is to inspire the individual member to think about, feel about, and then do something about gospel truths and principles. To do this, we must and will develop great teachers in the Church.

Harold B. Lee

Four goals of an effective teacher are: (1) to inspire; (2) to instruct; (3) to illustrate; and (4) to ignite.

A teacher affects eternity; he can never tell where his influence stops.

Henry Brooks Adams

Helps for Leadership

The great influencing factor in the classroom is the teacher, his personality, what he thinks — not just what he says, but what he is, really and truly, in his heart. This is what influences his students.

I hear and I forget; I see and I remember; I do and I understand.

As the individual in the large corporation becomes increasingly nameless and faceless, leadership traits and the ability to distinguish them grow more important. The successful leader combines these four qualities:

1. He has faith in himself and his followers, but this faith is never dogmatic. He is direct but not tactless, neither self-conscious nor oversensitive.

2. He is open-minded, interested in participating in and being part of the group. He combines perspective with the least possible prejudice.

3. The third quality, single-mindedness, is equivalent to mental integrity. He has a singleness of purpose and a desire to complete the tasks assigned to him. He's consistent but not rigid.

4. Responsibility is intimately involved with the other three qualities and is really an intellectual attitude. The reasons for his actions are clear to himself and his followers, and his goals are soundly based. He possesses a healthy optimism with a rational outlook and is ready to take the blame for his failures.

Actually, these traits are simply the qualities of a mature individual.

◆

SUGGESTIONS FOR SUCCESSFUL INTERVIEWS

1. Be available.
2. Be interested.
3. Be friendly.
4. Be watchmen on the towers of Zion.
5. Be specific.
6. Be thorough.
7. Be confidential.
8. Be a good listener.
9. Be in tune with the Spirit.

◆

Ivy Lee, a management consultant, created a $25,000 idea that can apply to leadership. He suggests that you

1. make a list of the six most important things you need to do tomorrow;
2. determine the relative importance of the six items and number them in order of importance;
3. tackle one at a time each of the items in order of importance. Stay with #1 until it is finished. Then do item #2, item #3, and so on until they are finished. Do this until the allotted time is gone. Maybe you will not finish all of the items listed. Don't be concerned about this, because you know you are working on the important ones. The others can wait;
4. spend the last five minutes of the time set aside making out a "must" list for the next work period. Do this every day.

◆

If you want something postponed, give it to a committee.

Charles Franklin Kettering

◆

Helps for Leadership

The late Jacob D. Cox, Jr., formerly president of Cleveland Twist Drill Company, used to tell the following story:

Jimmy Green was a new union committee member who stopped in to see Mr. Cox after contract negotiations had been concluded. Jimmy said that every other place he had worked he had always gone home grouchy; he never wanted to play with the children or take his wife to the movies. And then Jimmy said, "But since I have been working here, all that has changed. Now when I come home, the children run to meet me, and we have a grand romp together. It is a wonderful difference, and I don't know why; but I thought you would like to know."

As Mr. Cox observed, there must be a lot of Jimmy Greens in the world who want an opportunity to take part freely in a cooperative effort that has a moral purpose.

O. A. Ohmann

A good leader takes a little more than his share of the blame and a little less than his share of the credit.

Arnold H. Glasow

If you would become a leader, be prepared to assume heavy responsibility and take a lot of thoughtless, unjust criticism.

A pioneer is one who goes before, showing others the way to follow.

◆

On the wall of the Engineering Society Library in New York is the following inscription: "Management is the art and science of preparing, organizing and directing human effort applied to control the forces and utilize the materials of nature for the benefit of man."

◆

Who touches a boy by the Master's plan
Is shaping the course of a future man,
Is dealing with one who is living seed
And may be a man whom the world will need.

◆

A psychologist by the name of J. W. Bagby of New York's Roosevelt Hospital asked American and Mexican school teachers to look into a device that showed simultaneously a different picture to each eye. One eye of each person who looked into the device was shown a picture of a baseball player, and the other eye was shown a picture of a bullfighter. After they had been shown the two simultaneous pictures, they were asked what they saw. An overwhelming proportion of the Mexicans "saw" the bullfighter. What those teachers saw, of course, was mostly determined by their cultural filter. It was a test to prove that we see things in terms of our conditioning.

Earl Nightingale

◆

A leader needs to follow a line of action and thought that will lead him to make right decisions: get the facts, weigh and appraise, take action, and check results.

Royal Bank of Canada Newsletter

◆

---◆---

Guiding missiles is the work of scientists. Our task is the guiding of souls.

---◆---

A DOZEN RULES FOR
THE EMPLOYEE ON THE WAY UP

1. Don't let your boss be surprised.
2. Admit your mistakes frankly and promptly.
3. Have a recommendation ready.
4. Have at least one alternate plan.
5. If you don't know, admit it.
6. Have the facts and figures ready.
7. Make it a rule to date everything.
8. Don't pass the buck — grab it.
9. Pass along all good suggestions.
10. Write one-page memos.
11. Don't be afraid to train an understudy.
12. Try on your boss's problems.

---◆---

No organization can take men's time unless it lifts men's lives.

---◆---

Mr. George Spatta of Clark Equipment Company, when asked what he looks for in an executive, replied: "One who has ability to think clearly, has knowledge of the job, is a hard worker and can get along with others."

---◆---

What is the executive's most fundamental task? It is to deal with change.

---◆---

The real qualities of leadership are found in those who are willing to sacrifice for the sake of objectives great enough to demand their wholehearted allegiance. Simply holding a position of leadership does not make a man a leader. If you would be a real leader, you must endure loneliness. If you would be a real leader, you must endure weariness. Leadership requires vision.

A real leader ought to be able to foresee what his policies will do to the next generation. Vision must have hope and optimism in it. The past must push us — never pull us.

Clarence F. Sharer

A leader must realize that he is in a position to set an example and must deny himself, therefore, many of the privileges of a follower. Further, he must realize that, as he progresses to positions of increasing leadership, he must continue to study, train, and practice. His efforts to develop himself must be unceasing if he is to meet the challenge of leadership.

Gordon Ellis

The executive who is concerned with what a man cannot do rather than what he can do and therefore tries to avoid weakness rather than make strength effective is probably weak himself. He probably sees strength in others as a threat to himself. But no executive has ever suffered because his subordinates were strong and effective.

Peter Drucker

Helps for Leadership

————————◆————————

Hearts will inspire other hearts with their fire; for the strong obey when a strong man shows them the way.

Sigmund Romberg

————————◆————————

Always show your customer what your product can do for him.

Amos Parrish
Advertising Executive

————————◆————————

From my years of experience, I have come to this conclusion: Management simply must get more information. Our people have more valuable information than one thinks.

Stephen R. Covey

————————◆————————

The most valuable of all capital is that invested in human beings.

Alfred Marshall

————————◆————————

It was reported that one bishop formed the habit of going down to the railroad station every morning to see the train pull out. Someone asked him why, and he said that it just made him feel so good to see something move on its own power without his having to push it.

Sterling W. Sill

————————◆————————

Those who believe that might is right must always be mighty.

Ken Follett

"Follow the Leader" is more than a game when we remember that the power to lead is the power to mislead, and the power to mislead is the power to destroy.

Thomas S. Monson

Striving
for
Exaltation

Striving
for
Exaltation

---◆---

Men not unfrequently forget that they are dependent upon heaven for every blessing which they are permitted to enjoy, and that for every opportunity granted them they are to give an account. You know . . . that when the Master, in the Savior's parable of the stewards, called his servants before him, he gave them several talents to improve on while he should tarry abroad for a little season, and when he returned, he called for an accounting. So it is now. Our Master is absent only for a little season, and at the end of it He will call each to render an account.

Joseph Smith

---◆---

If we get puffed up by thinking that we have much knowledge, we are apt to get a contentious spirit.

Joseph Smith

---◆---

Inscription on the wall of the Library of Congress: "Beauty is truth; truth is beauty."

---◆---

The nearer a person approaches the Lord, the greater power will be manifest by the Adversary to prevent the accomplishment of his purposes.

Heber C. Kimball

Alcohol demoralizes those who make it, those who sell it, and those who drink it.

Robert Ingersoll

"Be ye angry, and sin not: let not the sun go down upon your wrath."

Ephesians 4:26

A great virtue in having a sense of values is that you have a compass you can trust. When Francis Chichester crossed the Atlantic in mid-1962 he was alone in his twenty-eight-foot sailboat, and all around him the sea met the sky in an unmarked horizon. But he was not lost. He had a compass; his course was charted; the stars were overhead.

Royal Bank of Canada Newsletter

The Lord God gave unto man that he should act for himself. "Wherefore, men are free according to the flesh; . . . they are free to choose liberty and eternal life, through the great Mediator of all men, or to choose captivity and death, according to the captivity and power of the devil."

2 Nephi 2:27

"Believe in God, . . . that he created all things. . . ; believe that he has all wisdom, and all power, . . . Believe that ye must repent of your sins and forsake them, and humble yourselves before God; . . . if you believe all these things see that ye do them."

Mosiah 4:9-10

"Know ye not that ye are the temple of God, and that the Spirit of God dwelleth in you?"

1 Corinthians 3:16

"Prepare to die" is not the exhortation of this Church and Kingdom, but "prepare to live." Then let us seek to extend present life to the uttermost.

Brigham Young

"For behold, the Spirit of Christ is given to every man, that he may know good from evil; wherefore, I show unto you the way to judge; for every thing which inviteth to do good, and to persuade to believe in Christ, is sent forth by the power and gift of Christ; wherefore ye may know with a perfect knowledge it is of God.

"But whatsoever thing persuadeth men to do evil, and believe not in Christ, and deny him, and serve not God, then ye may know with a perfect knowledge it is of the devil."

Moroni 7:16-17

A sense of values is needed in private life as well as in the marketplace. All our lives we are exercising choices, preferring this to that, deciding between better and worse.

Life would be uninteresting and drab if we did not set for ourselves certain goals and commit ourselves to some method for keeping score.

I would rather walk barefoot all the way to the Celestial Kingdom than to let the things of this world keep me out of that kingdom.

N. Eldon Tanner

In this day when modesty is thrust into the background and chastity is considered an outmoded virtue, I appeal to you to keep your souls unmarred and unsullied from this sin, "the prostitution of love," the consequence of which will smite and haunt you intimately until your conscience is seared and your character sordid.

David O. McKay

CHOOSE THE RIGHT

Choose the right! there is peace in righteous doing;
Choose the right! there's safety for the soul;
Choose the right in all labors you're pursuing;
Let God and heaven be your goal.

Joseph L. Townsend

88

Striving for Exaltation

The Savior's refusal to misuse his power guaranteed the continuance of his power.

Hugh B. Brown

"Behold, I am Jesus Christ, whom the prophets testified shall come into the world. . . . I am the light and the life of the world. . . . Whoso believeth in me, and is baptized, the same shall be saved; and they are they who shall inherit the kingdom of God."

3 Nephi 11:10-11,33

"In the world ye shall have tribulation: but be of good cheer; I have overcome the world."

John 16:33

The prophet Joseph Smith set forth the purpose of the Church when he declared: "It is the bringing of men and women to a knowledge of the eternal truth that Jesus is the Christ, the Redeemer and Savior of the world, and that only through belief in Him and faith which manifests itself in good works, can men and nations enjoy peace."

The sturdy discipline of intimate friendship with Jesus results in men becoming like Him.

Harry Emerson Fosdick

The recognition of a power higher than man, himself, does not in any sense debase him. If, in his faith, he ascribes beneficence and high purpose to the Power which is superior to himself, he envisions a higher destiny and nobler attributes for his kind and is stimulated and encouraged in the struggle for existence.

He must seek, believing, praying, and hoping that he will find. No such sincere, prayerful effort will go unrequited—that is the very constitution of the philosophy of faith.

Divine favor will attend those who humbly seek it.

Stephen L Richards

Would you judge the lawfulness or unlawfulness of pleasure? Then use this rule: Whatever weakens your reason, impairs the tenderness of your conscience, obscures your sight of God, takes from you your thirst for spiritual things or increases the authority of your body over your mind, then that thing to you is evil. By this test you may detect evil no matter how subtly or how plausibly temptation may be presented to you.

Susannah Wesley
Mother of reformist John Wesley

Faith and doubt cannot exist in the mind at the same time, for one will dispel the other.

Charles S. Hyde

"We walk by faith, not by sight."

2 Corinthians 5:7

90

A PLEDGE OF CHRISTIANITY

I will learn;
I will love;
I will serve;
I will obey.

Should the commandments of God be rewritten?
No—reread and, I might add, relived.

Richard L. Evans

O LITTLE TOWN OF BETHLEHEM

O little town of Bethlehem,
How still we see thee lie!
Above thy deep and dreamless sleep
The silent stars go by.
Yet in the dark streets shineth
The everlasting Light;
The hopes and fears of all the years
Are met in thee tonight.

How silently, how silently,
The wondrous Gift is given!
So God imparts to human hearts
The blessings of His heaven.
No ear may hear His coming,
But in this world of sin,
Where meek souls will receive Him, still
The dear Christ enters in.

Phillips Brooks

———————————◆———————————

I shall never believe that God plays dice with the world.

Albert Einstein

———————————◆———————————

THE CONQUERERS

Jesus and Alexander died at thirty-three.
One lived and died for self; one died for you and me.
The Greek died on a throne; the Jew died on a cross.
One's life a triumph seemed, the other but a loss.
One led vast armies forth, the other walked alone;
One shed a whole world's blood, the other gave His own.
One won the world in life and lost it all in death;
The other lost His life to win the whole world's faith.

Jesus and Alexander died at thirty-three.
One died in Babylon and one on Calvary.
One gained all for himself, and one Himself He gave.
One conquered every throne, the other every grave.
The one made himself a god, our God made Himself
the less.
The one lived but to blast, the other but to bless.
When died the Greek, forever fell his throne of swords;
But Jesus died to live forever Lord of lords.

Jesus and Alexander died at thirty-three.
The Greek made men slaves; the Jew made men free.
One built a throne on blood, the other built on love.
The one was born of earth, the other from above.
One won all this earth, to lose all earth and heaven.
The other gave up all, that all to Him be given.
The Greek forever died; the Jew forever lives.
He loses all who gets, and wins all things who gives.

Charles Ross Weede

———————————◆———————————

Our doubts are traitors,
And make us lose the good we oft might win,
By fearing to attempt.

William Shakespeare

"But I can't go on a mission to Canada, Brother Joseph," protested John E. Page. "I don't even have a coat to wear."

"Here," said Joseph Smith, removing his own coat, "take this, and the Lord will bless you."

THE DESERT

I said to a man who stood at the gate of the year:
"Give me a light that I may tread safely into the unknown."
And he replied:
"Go out into the darkness and put your hand into the hand
of God.
That shall be to you better than a light and safer than a
known way."
So I went forth and, finding the hand of God, trod gladly
into the night,
And He led me toward the hills and the breakings of day
in the lone East.

Minnie Louise Haskins

The Psalmist wrote ever so long ago: "It is better to trust in the Lord than to put confidence in man. It is better to trust in the Lord than to put confidence in princes."

Psalm 118:8-9

When I was in England many years ago, I purchased a book entitled *The Young Man and the World*. The book was written by the late senator from Indiana, Albert J. Beveridge. It was written originally as a series of contributions to *The Saturday Evening Post*, after which it was compiled in book form.

In one chapter, "The Young Man and the Pulpit," the author said that a certain individual with a very splendid opportunity of securing answers to interrogations, during an entire summer vacation asked every minister with whom he came in contact [two] questions:

First: *"Yes or no; do you believe in God the Father, God a person, God a definite and tangible intelligence — not a congeries of laws floating like a fog through the universe; but God, a person in whose image you were made? Don't argue; don't explain; but is your mind in a condition where you can answer yes or no?"*

Not a minister answered, "Yes," but they all gave a lot of explanations to the effect that we could not be sure about such things. . . .

The next question was: *"Yes or no; do you believe that Christ was the Son of the living God, sent by Him to save the world? I am not asking whether you believe that He was inspired in the sense that the great moral teachers are inspired — nobody has any difficulty about that. But do you believe that Christ was God's very Son, with a divinely appointed and definite mission, dying on the cross, and raised from the dead? Yes or no?"*

Again, not a single minister answered, "Yes." The sum total of their answers was that He was the greatest moral teacher that ever lived. I maintain that He could not possibly have been a moral teacher if He were not the Son of God, because that was the foundation of His teachings. He came as the Son of God to do the will of God, and He announced that

---

those who had seen Him had virtually seen God, because He was in the image of God.

Heber J. Grant

THE PACKAGE OF SEEDS

I paid a dime for a package of seeds
And the clerk tossed them out with a flip.
"We've got 'em assorted for every man's needs,"
He said with a smile on his lip,
"Pansies and poppies and asters and peas!
Ten cents a package! And pick as you please!"

Now seeds are just dimes to the man in the store,
And the dimes are the things that he needs;
And I've been to buy them in seasons before,
But have thought of them merely as seeds;
But it flashed through my mind as I took them this time,
"You have purchased a miracle here for a dime!"

"You've a dime's worth of power no man can create,
You've a dime's worth of life in your hand!
You've a dime's worth of mystery, destiny, fate,
Which the wisest cannot understand.
In this bright little package, now isn't it odd?
You've a dime's worth of something known only to God."

Edgar A. Guest

Only faith in a life after death, in a brighter world where dear ones will meet again—only that and the measured tramp of time can give consolation.

Sir Winston Churchill

God left the world unfinished for man to work his skill upon. He left the electricity still in the cloud, the oil still in the earth. He left the rivers unbridged and the forests unfelled and cities unbuilt. God gave to man the challenge of raw materials—not the ease of finished things. He left the pictures unpainted and the music unsung and the problems unsolved, that man might know the joys and glories of creation.

This is Lincoln's statement of faith formulated by Dr. William E. Barton from the martyred president's own words:

I believe in penitential and pious sentiments, in devotional designs and purposes, in homages and confessions, in supplications to the Almighty, solemnly, earnestly, reverently.

I believe in blessings and comfort from the Father of Mercies to the sick, the wounded, the prisoners, and to the orphans and widows.

I believe it pleases Almighty God to prolong our national life, defending us with His guardian care.

I believe in His eternal truth and justice.

I believe the will of God prevails; without Him all human reliance is vain; without the assistance of that Divine Being I cannot succeed; with that assistance I cannot fail.

I believe I am a humble instrument in the hands of our Heavenly Father; I desire that all my works and acts may be according to His will; and that it may be so, I give thanks to the Almighty and seek His aid.

I believe in praise to Almighty God, the beneficent Creator and Ruler of the Universe.

A BAG OF TOOLS

Isn't it strange that princes and kings
And clowns that caper in sawdust rings,
And simple folks like you and me
Are builders for eternity?

To each is given a bag of tools,
A shapeless mass and a set of rules;
And each must make, e're life has flown,
A stumbling block or a stepping stone.

R. L. Sharpe

How oft have wise men and women sought to dictate
Brother Joseph by saying, "O, if I were Brother Joseph I
would do this and that;" but if they were in Brother Joseph's
shoes they would find that men or women could not be
compelled into the kingdom of God, but must be dealt with
in long-suffering, and at last we shall save them.

Joseph Smith

The smile of God's approval is the greatest of all gifts.

RETRIBUTION

Though the mills of God grind slowly,
Yet they grind exceeding small;
Though with patience He stands waiting,
With exactness grinds He all.

Friedrich von Logau

GOD OF OUR FATHERS, KNOWN OF OLD

God of our fathers, known of old,
Lord of our far-flung battleline,
Beneath whose awful hand we hold
Dominion over palm and pine,
Lord God of Hosts, be with us yet,
Lest we forget, lest we forget!

The tumult and the shouting dies,
The captains and the kings depart;
Still stands thine ancient sacrifice,
An humble and a contrite heart;
Lord God of Hosts, be with us yet,
Lest we forget, lest we forget!

Far-called, our navies melt away,
On dune and headland sinks the fire;
Lo, all our pomp of yesterday
Is one with Nineveh and Tyre!
Judge of the nations, spare us yet,
Lest we forget, lest we forget!

Rudyard Kipling

[The gift of the Holy Ghost] is necessary to make and to organize the Priesthood. . . . No man can be called to fill any office in the ministry without it; we also believe in prophecy, in tongues, in visions, and in revelations, in gifts, and in healings; and . . . these things cannot be enjoyed without the gift of the Holy Ghost.

Joseph Smith

98

ODE

Our birth is but a sleep and a forgetting:
The soul that rises with us, our life's star,
Hath had elsewhere its setting,
And cometh from afar:
Not in entire forgetfulness,
And not in utter nakedness,
But trailing clouds of glory do we come
From God, who is our home:
Heaven lies about us in our infancy!

William Wordsworth

On May 8, 1838, Joseph Smith was desirous of setting forth the answers to questions which had been presented to him over and over again. To one of these questions he replied as follows:

Question: What are the fundamental principles of your religion?

Answer: The fundamental principles of our religion are the testimony of the Apostles and Prophets concerning Jesus Christ: that He died, was buried and rose again the third day and ascended into heaven; and all other things which pertain to our religion are only appendages to it.

William Gladstone described as the world's greatest need: "A living faith in a personal God."

Today, more than ever before, our survival—yours and mine and our children's—depends on our adherence to ethical principles. Ethics alone will decide whether atomic energy will be an earthly blessing or the source of mankind's utter destruction.

Where does the desire for ethical action come from? What makes us want to be ethical? I believe there are two forces which move us. One is belief in a Last Judgment, when every one of us has to account for what we did with God's great gift of life on the earth. The other is belief in an immortal soul, a soul which will cherish the award or suffer the penalty decreed in a final Judgment.

Belief in God and in immortality thus gives us the moral strength and the ethical guidance we need for virtually every action in our daily lives. In our modern world many people seem to feel that science has somehow made such "religious ideas" untimely or old-fashioned. But I think science has a real surprise for the skeptics. Science, for instance, tells us that nothing in nature, not even the tiniest particle, can disappear without a trace. Think about that for a moment. Once you do, your thoughts about life will never be the same.

Science has found that nothing can disappear without a trace. Nature does not know extinction. All it knows is transformation!

Now, if God applies this fundamental principle to the most minute and insignificant parts of His universe, doesn't it make sense to assume that He applies it also to the masterpiece of His creation: the human soul? I think it does. And everything science has taught me—and continues to teach me—strengthens my belief in the continuity of our spiritual existence after death. Nothing disappears without a trace.

Dr. Wernher von Braun

LEAD, KINDLY LIGHT

Lead, kindly Light, amid the encircling gloom;
Lead thou me on!
The night is dark, and I am far from home;
Lead thou me on!
Keep thou my feet; I do not ask to see
The distant scene — one step enough for me.

I was not ever thus, nor prayed that thou
Shouldst lead me on;
I loved to choose and see my path; but now
Lead thou me on!
I loved the garish day, and, spite of fears,
Pride ruled my will. Remember not past years.

So long thy power hath blest me, sure it still
Will lead me on
O'er moor and fen, o'er crag and torrent, till
The night is gone,
And with the morn those angel faces smile,
Which I have loved long since, and lost awhile!

John Henry Newman

How far is heaven?
It's not very far.
With people like you,
It's right where you are.

"Children, obey your parents in all things: for this is well pleasing unto the Lord."

Colossians 3:20

"If you will that I give unto you a place in the celestial world, you must prepare yourselves by doing the things which I have commanded you. "

D&C 78:7

When the moment for decision arrives, the time for preparation is past.

Thomas S. Monson

In *A Man for All Seasons*, Thomas More converses with Richard Rich, an ambitious young intellectual who ultimately betrays More and who loses his soul by selling out to ambition. More, who intuits Rich's problems and probable future, has told him to be satisfied with being a teacher; he can be a fine one. Rich asks who would *know* it if he were, and More replies, "You, your students, your friends, God. Not a bad public, that."

If I could choose what of all things would be at the same time the most delightful and useful to me, I should prefer a firm religious belief to every other blessing.

Sir Humphrey Davy

I believe . . . that the soul of Man is immortal and will be treated with justice in another life respecting its conduct in this.

Benjamin Franklin

Imagine yourself as a living house. God comes in to rebuild that house. At first, perhaps, you can understand what He is doing. He is getting the drains right and stopping the leaks in the roof and so on. He knew that those jobs needed doing and so you were not surprised. But presently He starts knocking the house about in a way that hurts and does not seem to make sense. What on earth is He up to? The explanation is that He is building quite a different house from the one you thought of—throwing out a new wing here, putting on an extra floor there, running up towers, making courtyards. You thought you were going to be made into a decent little cottage; but He is building a palace.

C. S. Lewis

Moral decay and religious principle are like twin buckets in a well. When one goes up, the other goes down. When religion declines, immorality inevitably will be on the rise.

Richard Wiley

Hope is the anchor of life. Religious hope is that and, we might add, also the wind and the sail.

"For all who will have a blessing at my hands shall abide the law which was appointed for that blessing, and the conditions thereof, as were instituted from before the foundation of the world."

D&C 132:5

---◆---

We carry upon our shoulders the reputation of the
Church—each and every one of us.

Heber J. Grant

---◆---

Thomas Carlyle made the following comment of his own
hometown: "This community needs a man who knows God
other than by hearsay."

---◆---

A test whereby we can know whether or not revelation is
from God:
1. Is it contrary to instruction from a living Prophet?
2. Is there anything secret?
3. Does it bring harmony and peace of mind?
4. Does it square with the scriptures?
5. What have you done yourself to ask of the Lord?
6. Are you keeping the commandments?
By answering this series of questions, you can know by the
Spirit whether or not the information comes from God.

---◆---

Wouldst thou be gathered to Christ's chosen flock? Shun
the broad way too easily explored. And let thy path be
hewn out of the rock—the living rock of God's eternal word.

William Wordsworth

---◆---

One, on God's side, is a majority.

Wendell Phillips

---◆---

Striving for Exaltation

I am one of those who believes that all institutions and organizations exist primarily for the purpose of securing to the individual his rights, his happiness, and proper development of his character. As soon as organizations fail to accomplish this purpose, their usefulness ceases.

Jesus always sought the welfare of the individual, and individuals grouped and laboring for the mutual welfare of the whole in conformity with the principles of the gospel constitute the Kingdom of God.

To the members of The Church of Jesus Christ of Latter-day Saints, the worth of the individual has special meaning. Quorums, auxiliaries, wards, stakes, even the Church itself, are all organized to further the welfare of man. All are but means to an end, and that end is the happiness and eternal welfare of every child of God.

David O. McKay

They who know the truth are not so great as they who love it; and they who love the truth are not so great as they who live it.

Chinese Proverb

"And we did magnify our office unto the Lord, taking upon us the responsibility, answering the sins of the people upon our own heads if we did not teach them the word of God with all diligence; wherefore, by laboring with our might their blood might not come upon our garments . . . , and we would not be found spotless at the last day."

Jacob 1:19

◆

The time has come to cease emphasizing the gadgets of everyday living and to set over against them the imperishable qualities of honesty, integrity, unselfishness, and respect for law.

◆

"There is a law, irrevocably decreed in heaven before the foundations of this world, upon which all blessings are predicated — and when we obtain any blessings from God, it is by obedience to that law upon which it is predicated."

D&C 130:20-21

◆

"I, the Lord, am bound when ye do what I say; but when ye do not what I say, ye have no promise."

D&C 82:10

◆

In a welfare meeting of the Monument Park West Stake, Elder Paul C. Child of the Welfare Committee asked the question: "What is the worth of a soul?"

One in the audience gave a rather interesting answer: "The worth of a soul is its capacity to become as God."

◆

"Organize yourselves; prepare every needful thing; and establish a house, even a house of prayer, a house of fasting, a house of faith, a house of learning, a house of glory, a house of order, a house of God."

D&C 88:119

◆

———————————◆———————————

The knights of France and England wrote this into their code of chivalry whereby they spurred themselves to heroic and generous actions: Courage is splendid, fidelity is noble, distressed people should be rescued, and vanquished enemies should be spared.

———————————◆———————————

In our quest for knowledge, there is no room for cheating, for dishonesty or that which would degrade us or cause the loss of our precious self-respect. In decision making we ask not "What will others think?" but "What will I think of myself?"

———————————◆———————————

MY CREED

I would be true,
   for there are those who trust me;
I would be pure,
   for there are those who care;
I would be strong,
   for there is much to suffer;
I would be brave,
   for there is much to dare.
I would be friend of all —
   the foe, the friendless;
I would be giving,
   and forget the gift;
I would be humble,
   for I know my weakness;
I would look up — and laugh —
   and love — and lift.

Howard Arnold Walter

———————————◆———————————

Of all the acts of man, repentance is the most divine. The greatest of faults, I should say, is to be conscious of none.

Thomas Carlyle

You cannot repent too soon, because you do not know how soon it may be too late.

Thomas Fuller

We must not insist on remembering what God has indicated He is willing to forget.

Hugh B. Brown

Money is not required to buy one necessity of the soul.

Henry David Thoreau

Do not pray for tasks equal to your powers. Pray for powers equal to your tasks. Then the doing of your work shall be no miracle, but you shall be the miracle.

Thomas S. Monson

"The Lord appeared to Solomon . . . and the Lord said unto him, I have heard thy prayer and thy supplication, that thou hast made before me: I have hallowed this house, which thou hast built, to put my name there for ever; and mine eyes and mine heart shall be there perpetually."

1 Kings 9:2-3

"Create in me a clean heart, O God; and renew a right spirit within me. Cast me not away from thy presence; and take not thy holy spirit from me. Restore unto me the joy of thy salvation; and uphold me with thy free spirit."

Psalm 51:10

REVELATION

I knelt to pray when day was done.
And prayed, "O Lord, bless everyone;
Lift from each saddened heart the pain
And let the sick be well again."
And then I woke another day
And carelessly went on my way.
The whole day long I did not try
To wipe a tear from any eye;
I did not try to share the load
Of any brother on my road;
I did not even go to see
The sick man just next door to me.
Yet once again when day was done
I prayed, "O Lord, bless everyone."
But as I prayed, into my ear
There came a voice that whispered clear:
"Pause, hypocrite, before you pray,
Whom have you tried to bless today?
God's sweetest blessings always go
By hands that serve Him here below."
And then I hid my face, and cried,
"Forgive me, God, for I have lied;
Let me but see another day
And I will live the way I pray."

Whitney Montgomery

109

I believe in prayer, and I pray.

David M. Kennedy
Former U. S. Secretary of the Treasury

My words fly up, my thoughts remain below:
Words without thoughts never to heaven go.

William Shakespeare

There is no act of a Latter-day Saint, no duty required, no time given, exclusive and independent of the priesthood. Everything is subject to it, whether preaching, business, or any other act pertaining to the proper conduct of this life.

Brigham Young

The greatest force in this world today is the power of God as it works through man.

It is your duty first of all to learn what the Lord wants and then by the power and strength of your holy priesthood to so magnify your calling in the presence of your fellows that the people will be glad to follow you.

George Albert Smith

If you find yourself further away from God than you were yesterday, you can be sure who has moved.

Striving for Exaltation

If I had been set to turn the world over, to dig down a mountain, to go to the ends of the earth, or traverse the deserts of Arabia, it would have been easier to have undertaken to rest while the priesthood was upon me. I have received the holy annointing, and I can never rest until the last enemy is conquered, death destroyed, and truth reigns triumphant.

Parley P. Pratt

AN ESSAY ON MAN

Vice is a monster of so frightful mien,
As to be hated needs but to be seen;
Yet seen too oft, familiar with her face,
We first endure, then pity, then embrace.

Alexander Pope

Neglect of opportunity in holy things develops inability.

James E. Talmage

There was never yet a truly great man who was not at the same time truly virtuous.

Benjamin Franklin

We are not teaching lessons; we are preparing for a temptation which will surely come.

Harold B. Lee

◆

TO A WATERFOWL

Whither, midst falling dew,
While glow the heavens with the last steps of day,
Far, through their rosy depth, dost thou pursue
Thy solitary way?

Vainly the fowler's eye
Might mark thy distant flight to do thee wrong,
As, darkly painted on the crimson sky,
Thy figure floats along.

Seek'st thou the plashy brink
Of weedy lake, or marge of river wide,
Or where the rocking billows rise and sink
On the chafed ocean-side?

All day thy wings have fanned
At that far height, the cold, thin atmosphere,
Yet stoop not, weary, to the welcome land,
Though the dark night is near.

And soon that toil shall end;
Soon shalt thou find a summer home, and rest,
And scream among thy fellows; reeds shall bend,
Soon, o'er thy sheltered nest.

He who, from zone to zone,
Guides through the boundless sky that certain flight,
In the long way that I must tread alone,
Will lead my steps aright.

William Cullen Bryant

◆

"The heavens declare the glory of God; and the firmament sheweth his handywork."

Psalm 19:1

◆

112

It matters not what else we have been called to do or what position we may occupy or how faithfully in other ways we have labored in the Church; none is exempt from the great obligation of performance of temple work for the dead. It is required of the Apostles as well as of the humblest Elder. Place or distinction or long service in the Church, in the mission fields, the stakes of Zion or where or how else it may have been, will not entitle one to disregard the salvation of one's dead. Some may feel that if they pay their tithing, attend to their regular meetings and other duties, give of their substance to feed the poor, perchance spend one or two years preaching in the world that they are absolved from further duty. But the greatest and grandest duty of all is to labor for the dead. We may and should do all these other things for which reward will be given, but if we neglect the work for the dead, all our other good works notwithstanding, we shall find ourselves under severe condemnation.

Joseph Fielding Smith

Why is not God already real to Americans who are among the most church-going people in the world? Partly because of the blight of secularism in the churches, which have become just another valued branch of American democratic culture instead of its center. What used to be the minister's study is now his office, and as a busy agent of the social gospel, he is less a spokesman of God than a useful citizen, making East Overshoe "a better place to live." A society that apotheocizes techniques and talks more about its processes than its aims has made God Himself a technique instead of the source and goal of our being.

Life

"For where your treasure is, there will your heart be also."

Matthew 6:21

"With my whole heart I have sought thee: O let me not wander from thy commandments."

Psalm 119:10

If you want to know what the Lord has for this people at the present time, I would admonish you to get and read the discourses that have been delivered at this conference; for what these brethren have spoken by the power of the Holy Ghost is the mind of the Lord, the will of the Lord, the voice of the Lord, and the power of God unto salvation.

Harold B. Lee

"Lord, who shall abide in thy tabernacle? who shall dwell in thy holy hill? He that walketh uprightly, and worketh righteousness, and speaketh the truth in his heart."

Psalm 15:1-2

"Out of the abundance of the heart the mouth speaketh."

Matthew 12:34

Striving for Exaltation

"Let the words of my mouth, and the meditation of my heart, be acceptable in thy sight, O Lord, my strength, and my redeemer."

Psalm 19:14

We should avail ourselves of those sacred and potent ordinances of the Gospel which have been revealed as essential to the happiness, salvation and redemption of those who have lived in this world when they could not live the Gospel and have died without the knowledge of it, and are now waiting for us, their children, who are living in an age when these ordinances can be performed, to do the work necessary for their release from the prison house. Through our efforts in their behalf, their chains of bondage will fall from them, and the darkness surrounding them will clear away, that light may shine upon them and they shall hear in the spirit world of the work that has been done for them by their children here, and will rejoice with you in your performance of these duties.

Joseph F. Smith

"Whatsoever thing is good is just and true; wherefore, nothing that is good denieth the Christ, but acknowledgeth that he is."

Moroni 10:6

"Attend to my words; incline thine ear unto my sayings. Let them not depart from thine eyes; keep them in the midst of thine heart."

Proverbs 4:20-21

"And when ye shall receive these things, I would exhort you that ye would ask God, the Eternal Father, in the name of Christ, if these things are not true; and if ye shall ask with a sincere heart, with real intent, having faith in Christ, he will manifest the truth of it unto you, by the power of the Holy Ghost."

Moroni 10:4

"Yea, behold, I will tell you in your mind and in your heart, by the Holy Ghost, which shall come upon you and which shall dwell in your heart."

D&C 8:2

Man has changed again and again, but the mandates from God are still the same as they have always been because the fundamental principles of good behavior are immutable.

David Lawrence

Family prayer is the greatest deterrent to sin and thence the most beneficent provider of joy and happiness.

Striving for Exaltation

◆

OH SAY, WHAT IS TRUTH

Oh say, what is truth? 'Tis the fairest gem
That the riches of worlds can produce,
And priceless the value of truth will be when
The proud monarch's costliest diadem
Is counted but dross and refuse.

Yes, say, what is truth? 'Tis the brightest prize
To which mortals or Gods can aspire;
Go search in the depths where it glittering lies
Or ascend in pursuit to the loftiest skies:
'Tis an aim for the noblest desire.

The sceptre may fall from the despot's grasp
When with winds of stern justice he copes,
But the pillar of truth will endure to the last,
And its firm-rooted bulwarks outstand the rude blast,
And the wreck of the fell tyrant's hopes.

Then say, what is truth? 'Tis the last and the first,
For the limits of time it steps o'er.
Though the heavens depart and the earth's fountains burst,
Truth, the sum of existence, will weather the worst,
Eternal, unchanged, evermore.

John Jaques

◆

"The spirit and the body shall be reunited again in its
perfect form; both limb and joint shall be restored to its
proper frame, even as we now are. . . . Spirits uniting with
their bodies, never to be divided; thus, the whole becoming
spiritual and immortal."

Alma 11:43-45

◆

"God hath numbered thy kingdom, and finished it. . . . Thou art weighed in the balances, and art found wanting."

Daniel 5:26-27

In New York City on 5th Avenue and 65th Street is a Jewish Synagogue. On the exterior wall, chiseled in granite, are these two inscriptions: "Does justice love mercy?" "Walk humbly with thy God."

"After they had been received unto baptism, and were wrought upon and cleansed by the power of the Holy Ghost, they were numbered among the people of the church of Christ; and their names were taken, that they might be remembered and nourished by the good word of God, to keep them in the right way, to keep them continually watchful unto prayer, relying alone upon the merits of Christ, who was the author and the finisher of their faith."

Moroni 6:4

"The spirit and the body are the soul of man."

D&C 88:15

"Know ye not that your body is the temple of the Holy Ghost, which is in you, which ye have of God?"

1 Corinthians 6:19

118

Striving for Exaltation

◆

The purpose of the home teaching program is to have every member of every family do his duty.

Marion G. Romney

◆

Home teaching is missionary work to the member. Missionary work is home teaching to the nonmember.

Harold B. Lee

◆

Our central task [in home teaching] is to produce an individual who walks uprightly before the Lord.

David O. McKay

◆

It is a wise leader who follows the charted course, thereby eliminating errors and pitfalls. The captain of a ship would never put out to sea without a map and a compass. Nor would the pilot of a plane or an explorer in the jungle or arctic wastes set forth without the guidance of charts and maps. Where would the bus driver find himself if he just sallied forth aimlessly without direction?

The Lord has marked the path, and every point is defined for those to follow who would return unto Him. He has been very specific in His instructions, and they are well defined and available to us. He has told us that there is but one road, not many, to success (exaltation) and that this road is hard and difficult. "Strait is the gate and narrow is the way" are His words.

G. Carlos Smith, Jr.

◆

"Wide is the gate, and broad is the way, that leadeth to destruction, and many there be that go in thereat."

Matthew 7:13

THE VISION OF SIR LAUNFAL, PRELUDE

At the devil's booth are all things sold.
Each ounce of dross costs its ounce of gold.

James Russell Lowell

You will meet sin; shun it! You inherit freedom, protect it!
You have a testimony; share it! You know the truth; live it!

Thomas S. Monson

"He is the light and the life of the world; yea, a light that is endless, that can never be darkened; yea, and also a life which is endless, that there can be no more death. Even this mortal shall put on immortality, and this corruption shall put on incorruption, and shall be brought to stand before the bar of God, to be judged of him according to their works."

Mosiah 16:9-10

"In my Father's house are many mansions: if it were not so, I would have told you."

John 14:2

John Quincy Adams thus expressed his thoughts on immortality to a friend. When the friend inquired how he was, he replied:

> Thank you! John Quincy Adams himself is well, sir, quite well, I thank you. But the house in which he lives at present is becoming dilapidated. It is tottering upon its foundations. Time and the seasons have nearly destroyed it. The roof is pretty well worn out. Its walls are much shattered, and it trembles with every wind. The old tenement is becoming almost uninhabitable, and I think John Quincy Adams will have to move out of it soon; but he himself is quite well sir—quite well.

We have the Holy Ghost. Every one of us who is a member of the Church has had hands laid upon his head and has been given, as far as ordinances can give it, the gift of the Holy Ghost. But as I remember, when I was confirmed, the Holy Ghost was not directed to come to me. I was directed to "receive the Holy Ghost." If I receive the Holy Ghost and follow his guidance, I will be among those who are protected and carried through these troubled times. As so will you, and so will every soul who lives under his direction.

Marion G. Romney

No man for any considerable period can wear one face to himself and another to the multitude without finally getting bewildered as to which may be true.

Nathaniel Hawthorne

The Holy Ghost is the third member of the great trinity, the Godhead. He differs in some respects from the other two members. Our Father in Heaven, Elohim, and Jesus Christ, the Redeemer, have bodies of flesh and bone as tangible as man's. The Holy Ghost is a personage of spirit who has not a body of flesh and bones. His body is like the one Jesus had before He, Jesus, was born to Mary, the one we read about in the book of Ether, chapter 3.

These three—the Father, the Son, and the Holy Ghost—constitute the great governing council that controls the universe. One of the assignments of the Holy Ghost is to enlighten the minds of the believers in Christ. Those who accept His gospel, who repent and are baptized and receive the gift of the Holy Ghost by the ordinance of the laying on of hands, are given the right, based on continuous righteous living, to be guided by this third member of the Godhead, the Holy Ghost. He could come to one in person. He has the power to penetrate with his influence into the spirit and soul of every person in the earth. His power and influence go into every person in the earth who really accepts the Christ and complies with the principles and ordinances of His gospel. Such persons receive direction from that Holy Spirit, which guides them in their lives. That direction guides their thinking. It gives them strength, power, and knowledge. One who enjoys the gift of the Holy Ghost is brought back, to that extent, into the presence of God.

You can have the guidance of the Holy Spirit in selecting your profession or your vocation or whatever else you undertake to do in righteousness, if you are humble, live the standards that make us a peculiar people, and pray until you learn to talk with your God. The most valuable lesson you can learn in life is to be guided by the Holy Spirit.

Marion G. Romney

"If a person gains more knowledge and intelligence in this life through his diligence and obedience than another, he will have so much the advantage in the world to come."

D&C 130:19

"I saw the dead, small and great, stand before God; . . . the sea gave up the dead, which were in it; and death and hell delivered up the dead which were in them."

Revelation 20:12-13

"The spirits of all men, as soon as they are departed from this mortal body, yea, the spirits of all men, whether they be good or evil, are taken home to that God who gave them life. . . . The spirits of those who are righteous are received into a state of happiness, which is called paradise, a state of rest, a state of peace. . . . The spirits of the wicked . . . shall be cast out into outer darkness . . . a state of awful, fearful looking for the fiery indignation of the wrath of God upon them; thus they remain in this state, as well as the righteous in paradise, until the time of their resurrection."

Alma 40:11-14

"I am the resurrection, and the life: he that believeth in me, though he were dead, yet shall he live: And whosoever liveth and believeth in me shall never die."

John 11:25-26

◆

"Do we begin again to commend ourselves? or need we, as some others, epistles of commendation to you, or letters of commendation from you? Ye are our epistle written in our hearts, known and read of all men . . . , written not with ink, but with the Spirit of the living God; not in tables of stone, but in fleshy tables of the heart.

"[God] hath made us able ministers of the new testament; not of the letter, but of the spirit; for the letter killeth, but the spirit giveth life."

2 Corinthians 3:1-3,6

◆

The earth's a gentle place
When Spring first breathes anew,
And lifts its smiling face
To say that Winter's through.

The sun that paints the skies,
Which Winter grays conceal,
Bids nature to "Arise!"
And breaks the ice-tong's seal.

What song of hope is ours
As heaven's grace is shed
On hilltops crowned with flowers
That yesterday were dead?

The woodlands bleak and bare,
As death clutched every limb,
Now sanctify the air
With Resurrection's hymn.

Great signs that thrill the eyes!
How can they but impress?
If lowly plants must rise,
Should man expect much less?

Gerard Leo Tierney

◆

KNOW THIS, THAT EVERY SOUL IS FREE

Know this, that every soul is free
To choose his life and what he'll be;
For this eternal truth is given
That God will force no man to heav'n.

He'll call, persuade, direct aright,
And bless with wisdom, love, and light,
In nameless ways be good and kind,
But never force the human mind.

Anonymous

PRAYER

I know not by what methods rare
But this I know: God answers prayer.
I know that He has given His word
Which tells me prayer is always heard
And will be answered, soon or late,
And so I pray and calmly wait.
I know not if the blessings sought
Will come just in the way I thought
But leave my prayers with Him alone
Whose will is wiser than my own,
Assured that He will grant my quest
Or send some answer far more blessed.

Eliza M. Hickok

Preparation
for
Achievement

---◆---

Preparation
for
Achievement

---◆---

It is better to be nobly remembered than nobly born.

John Ruskin

---◆---

As Theseus, King of Athens, said in one of Sophocles' plays:
"Nor am I careful to adorn my life with words of praise,
but with the light of deeds."

---◆---

One cannot get much satisfaction out of endless dreaming.
One must perform.

---◆---

Our circle of concern is greater than our circle of action.

---◆---

My life cannot implement in action the demands of all those
to whom my heart responds.

Anne Morrow Lindburgh

---◆---

THE QUITTER

Fate handed the quitter a bump, and he dropped;
The road seemed too rough to go, so he stopped.
He thought of his hurt, and there came to his mind
The easier path he was leaving behind.
"Oh, it's all much too hard," said the quitter right then;
"I'll stop where I am and not try it again."

He sat by the road and he made up his tale
To tell when men asked why he happened to fail.
A thousand excuses flew up to his tongue,
And these on the thread of his story he strung,
But the truth of the matter he didn't admit;
He never once said, "I was frightened and quit."

Whenever the quitter sits down by the road
And drops from the struggle to lighten his load,
He can always recall to his own peace of mind
A string of excuses for falling behind;
But somehow or other he can't think of one
Good reason for battling and going right on.

Oh, when the bump comes and fate hands you a jar,
Don't baby yourself, boy, whoever you are;
Don't pity yourself and talk over your woes;
Don't think up excuses for dodging the blows.
But stick to the battle and see the thing through.
And don't be a quitter, whatever you do.

Edgar A. Guest

If you could kick the person responsible for most of your troubles, you wouldn't be able to sit down for six months.

Gordon Gray

Preparation for Achievement

—————————◆—————————

To most of us the future seems unsure. But then, it always has been; and we who have seen great changes must have great hopes.

John Masefield

—————————◆—————————

THE MAN WHO THINKS HE CAN

If you think you are beaten, you are;
If you think you dare not, you don't.
If you like to win, but think you can't,
It's almost a cinch you won't.
If you think you'll lose, you're lost,
For out in the world we find
Success begins with a fellow's will;
It's all in the state of mind.

If you think you're outclassed, you are;
You've got to think high to rise.
You've got to be sure of yourself before
You can ever win a prize.
Life's battles don't always go
To the stronger or faster man;
But soon or late the man who wins
Is the man who thinks he can.

Walter D. Wintle

—————————◆—————————

When you are discouraged, look back carefully and honestly, and you will find that your work has not been done with all your might. Victory is bound to come to him who gives all of himself to the cause he represents, if there be truth in the cause.

—————————◆—————————

———————◆———————

Our business in life is not to get ahead of others but to get ahead of ourselves; to break our own records; to outstrip our yesterdays by our todays; to bear our trials more beautifully than we ever dreamed we could; to give as we never have given; to do our work with more force and a finer finish than ever. This is the true idea: to get ahead of ourselves.

Carl Holmes

———————◆———————

Men will work hard for money; they will work harder for other men. But men will work hardest of all when they are dedicated to a cause. Until willingness overflows obligation, men fight as conscripts rather than following the flag as patriots. Duty is never worthily performed until it is done by one who would gladly do more if he could.

Harry Emerson Fosdick

———————◆———————

I will do everything I can to serve you, and I will do everything I can to honor this high calling. God bless you, and God bless me, and will you please pray for me, that no enemy shall dent the small sector of the line which I am assigned to defend.

Marion G. Romney

———————◆———————

We should be painting a vastly greater mural on a vastly more spacious wall.

John Gardner

———————◆———————

Preparation for Achievement

THE WAYS

To every man there openeth
A Way, and Ways and a Way.
And the High Soul climbs the High Way,
And the Low Soul gropes the Low,
And in between, on the misty flats,
The rest drift to and fro.
But to every man there openeth
A High Way, and a Low,
And every man decideth
The way his soul shall go.

John Oxenham

Do we have good excuses for lack of achievement? History is replete with people with problems. Homer could have squatted at the gates of Athens, have been pitied and fed by coins from the rich. He, like Milton the poet and Prescott the historian, had a good alibi: he was blind, as were they. Demosthenes, greatest of all great orators, had a wonderful alibi: his lungs were weak, his voice hoarse and unmusical, and he stuttered. Julius Caesar, statesman and general, was an epileptic. Beethoven was stone deaf at middle age. They all had good alibis — but they never used them!

No power on earth can keep a first-class man down nor keep a fourth-class man up.

Have great dreams and dare to live them.

133

◆

THE MAN IN THE GLASS

When you get what you want in your struggle for self
And the world thinks you king for a day,
Just go to the mirror and look at yourself,
And see what *that* man has to say.

For it isn't your father, your mother, or wife
Who judgment upon you must pass;
The fellow whose verdict counts most in your life
Is the one staring back from the glass.

You may be like Jack Horner and chisel a plum
And think you're a wonderful guy;
But the man in the glass says you're only a bum
If you can't look him straight in the eye.

He's the fellow to please, never mind all the rest;
For he's with you clear to the end.
And you've passed your most dangerous, difficult test
If the man in the glass is your friend.

You may fool the whole world down the pathway of years
And get pats on the back as you pass;
But your final reward will be heartaches and tears
If you've cheated the man in the glass.

◆

William James announced the "as if" principle: If you want
a virtue, act as if you already have it. If you want to be
brave, act brave. Theodore Roosevelt was once decorating
one of his subordinates for bravery. He said in substance:
"This is the bravest man I have ever known. He was right
behind me all the way up San Juan Hill. That may sound
a little egotistical, but 'out of the abundance of the heart
the mouth speaketh,' and if you don't have it in you, you
can't get it out."

◆

Preparation for Achievement

Can Do will never fall down. He will always bring home the bacon. He will always keep us identified as our better self. *Can Do* knows his business; he keeps us at our peak of performance; he never has to be reminded or coaxed.

Sterling W. Sill

The man who swears allegiance to a cause places upon himself limitations beyond a slave because he has given his heart.

Harry Emerson Fosdick

Don't bring me your successes, for they weaken me; rather, bring me your problems, for they strengthen me.

Boss Kettering
Former president, General Motors

We cannot all be John Cabots, sailing off into the blue with the king's patent to discover new lands; but we can be explorers in spirit, with democracy's mandate to make this land better by discovering new ways of living and doing things.

The spirit of exploration, whether it be of the surface of the earth or the principles of living greatly, includes developing the capacity to face trouble with courage, disappointment with cheerfulness, and triumph with humility.

Royal Bank of Canada Newsletter

It's better to accomplish small tasks than to think great deeds.

During World War II, soldiers were asked to compete to see who had the most powerful grip. They averaged 101 pounds per man. Then they were hypnotized and given the negative suggestion that they were weak and sickly, feeble and anemic. They were told to grip the machine as tightly as they could. They averaged 69 pounds per man.

Before they were awakened from their hypnotic trance, they were given the positive message that they were Herculean, Samson-like and powerful. They were then told to grip the machine as tightly as they could. What do you think was the result? They now averaged 140 pounds per man. This more than doubled their 69 pound grip under the defeatist or negative attitude and was almost 40% better than their best record in the normal waking state.

Dr. George W. Crane

MR. MEANT-TO

Mr. Meant-to has a comrade,
And his name is Didn't-do.
Have you ever chanced to meet them?
Did they ever call on you?

These two fellows live together
In the house of Never-win,
And I'm told that it is haunted
By the ghost of Might-have-been.

Unknown

Preparation for Achievement

When I find out what the Lord wants me to do, I do it!

Joseph Smith

There is nothing we can't do in the building of the Lord's kingdom if we have the desire, do the work, and have the faith.

Henry D. Moyle

Ninety percent of our problems can be solved if we will but make up our minds.

Franklin D. Richards

A paralyzed woman who had lain for thirty years upon her bed, helpless but not hopeless, succeeding by a miracle of courage in her single aim — never complaining — always imparted a bit of her joy and peace to everyone who came near her.

God give us men! A time like this demands
Strong minds, great hearts, true faith, and ready hands.

Josiah Gilbert Holland

Remember that if we but have the right attitude, everything leaves us a blessing. No wind can blow except to fill our sails.

WORTH WHILE

It is easy enough to be pleasant
When life flows by like a song,
But the man worth while is one who will smile,
When everything goes dead wrong.
For the test of the heart is trouble,
And it always comes with the years,
And the smile that is worth the praises of earth
Is the smile that shines through tears.

It is easy enough to be prudent,
When nothing tempts you to stray,
When without or within no voice of sin
Is luring your soul away;
But it's only a negative virtue
Until it is tried by fire,
And the life that is worth the honor on earth
Is the one that resists desire.

By the cynic, the sad, the fallen,
Who had no strength for the strife,
The world's highway is cumbered to-day;
They make up the sum of life.
But the virtue that conquers passion,
And the sorrow that hides in a smile,
It is these that are worth the homage on earth,
For we find them but once in a while.

Ella Wheeler Wilcox

"Behold, the Lord requireth the heart and a willing mind;
and the willing and obedient shall eat the good of the land
of Zion in these last days."

D&C 64:34

Preparation for Achievement

The greatest discovery of my generation is that men can alter their lives by altering their attitudes of mind.

William James

IT SHOWS IN YOUR FACE

You don't have to tell how you live each day,
You don't have to say if you work or play,
A tried, true barometer serves in your place
However you live, it will show in your face.
The false, the deceit that you bear in your heart
Will not stay inside, where it first got a start.
For sinew and blood are a thin veil of lace,
What you wear in your heart you wear in your face.
If your life is unselfish, if for others you live
For not what you get, but for how much you can give,
If you live close to God, in His infinite grace,
You don't have to tell it, it shows in your face.

Unknown

YOU

You can do as much as you think you can,
But you'll never accomplish more;
If you're afraid of yourself, young man,
There's little for you in store.

For failure comes from the inside first;
It's there if you only knew it.
And you can win, though you face the worst,
If you feel you're going to do it!

Edgar A. Guest

NEWCASTLE, ENGLAND (UPI) — Fifteen-year-old
Michael Little gave a mighty heave Thursday and single-
handedly lifted a three-hundred-pound gate post which
had fallen on three-year-old Susan Brown. After freeing
the girl and seeing her safely off to the hospital in an
ambulance, the slim teenager tried to move the pillar to
clear the footpath it fell across. He had to call on two men
to help him budge it.

A soldier, prior to being killed in the first World War, wrote
in his diary: "I will work; I will save; I will sacrifice; I will
endure. I will serve cheerfully and do my utmost, as though
the entire conflict depended on me alone."

To pick up the pieces, to repair what is spoiled and start
over, is a noble act. John James Audubon, the ornithologist,
left a box containing two hundred of his beautiful drawings
at home when he went on a business trip. Upon his return
he found that a pair of rats had entered the box and gnawed
the paper on which he had drawn a thousand birds.
Audubon was prostrated for several days by the shock; then
he took up his notebook and pencils and went out into the
woods. "I felt pleased," he said, "that I might now make
better drawings than before."

Royal Bank of Canada Newsletter

The past is behind; learn from it.
The future is ahead; prepare for it.
The present is here; live in it!

Thomas S. Monson

Preparation for Achievement

───────◆───────

I don't go into a ball game just hoping to play a good ball game. I go into the ball game to try to win. They still keep score, don't they? As long as they keep score, someone is anxious to know how it is going to come out, and I am one of those anxious people.

Adolph Rupp
Kentucky University Coach

───────◆───────

You don't beat the best when he does not make a mistake.

Bruce Crampton

───────◆───────

Whether you think you can or whether you think you can't, you're right!

Henry Ford

───────◆───────

THE WINDS OF FATE

One ship drives east and another drives west
With the selfsame winds that blow.
'Tis the set of the sails
And not the gales
Which tell us the way to go.

Like the winds of the sea are the ways of fate,
As we voyage along through life:
'Tis the set of the soul
That decides the goal
And not the calm or the strife.

Ella Wheeler Wilcox

───────◆───────

———————————◆———————————

Socrates: "Know yourself." Cicero: "Control yourself." Jesus Christ: "Give yourself."

———————————◆———————————

Of this be sure: You do not find the happy life; you make it. If you could ascend to some great height giving a view of all the future landscape of your life, then you could recognize the best things afar off, and strike out for them. But since you cannot see very far ahead, you need to take each step with all the wisdom you can muster. While sensing what lies dimly ahead, you must do competently what lies clearly at hand.

Royal Bank of Canada Newsletter

———————————◆———————————

Everyone can be discontented if he ignores his blessings and looks only at his burdens.

———————————◆———————————

TEN COMMANDMENTS OF HOW TO GET ALONG WITH PEOPLE

1. Keep skid chains on your tongue; always say less than you think. Cultivate a low, persuasive voice. How you say it often counts more than what you say.

2. Make promises sparingly and keep them faithfully, no matter what it costs you.

3. Never let an opportunity pass to say a kind and encouraging thing to or about somebody. Praise good work done, regardless of who did it. If criticism is needed, criticize helpfully — never spitefully.

4. Be interested in others: interested in their welfare, their

———————————◆———————————

———————————◆———————————

homes, their families. Make merry with those who rejoice; with those who weep, mourn. Let everyone you meet, however humble, feel that you regard him as one of importance.

5. Be cheerful; keep the corners of your mouth turned up. Hide your pains, worries, and disappointments under a smile. Laugh at good stories and learn to tell them.

6. Preserve an open mind on all debatable questions. Discuss, but don't argue. It is a mark of superior minds to disagree and yet to be friendly.

7. Let your virtues, if you have any, speak for themselves, and refuse to talk of another's vices. Discourage gossip. Make it a rule to say nothing of another unless it is something good.

8. Be careful of another's feelings. Wit and humor at the other fellow's expense are rarely worth the effort and may hurt where least expected.

9. Pay no attention to ill-natured remarks about you. Simply live that nobody will believe them. Disordered nerves and a bad digestion are a common cause of backbiting.

10. Don't be too anxious about your dues. Do your work, be patient and keep your disposition sweet. Forget self, and you will be rewarded.

———————————◆———————————

"[Give] no offense in any thing, that the ministry be not blamed: but in all things [we should approve] ourselves as the ministers of God, in much patience."

2 Corinthians 6:3,4

———————————◆———————————

OMAHA, Neb., (UPI) — Arlan Greve said today that he was unable to explain how he managed to reach and rescue a three-year-old boy who was caught in his jacket and choking to death near the top of a backyard gymnasium set.

Greve, twenty-six years old, was crippled by poliomyelitis fifteen years ago and can walk only with crutches. Greve said he was leaning on a pair of crutches and looking out the back window of his home Thursday when he noticed Dean Alexis Zerbe hanging motionless from the gym set. Dean is the grandson of U. Alexis Johnson, United States Ambassador to Japan.

Greve yelled for help, but no one heard him. He then made his way through his yard to a wire fence separating his property from the home of Dean's parents, Mr. and Mrs. Mason Zerbe, Jr.

The gym set was close to the fence, but Greve could not reach it, he said. He tossed his crutches across and then he leaned backward against the fence until his weight plunged him into the Zerbe yard, he said.

Greve said the hood on the boy's jacket was caught near the top of the gym set and was choking him. "I don't know how I got up or got the boy down! I usually can't do that sort of thing," Greve said.

When he got him down, Greve said, the boy was blue-faced and stiff. He said the youngster had stopped breathing and that he could not detect a heartbeat.

Greve, a laboratory technician at Methodist Hospital here, began mouth-to-mouth resuscitation. When that failed, he switched to artificial respiration. Greve said he continued this for about fifteen minutes and continued yelling for help but got no response. When he was sure the boy was breathing well enough to be left alone briefly, Greve went

---

to the Zerbe home and called Mrs. Zerbe, who then telephoned for the rescue squad. She called neighbors also.

At Children's Hospital, from which Dean was released yesterday, doctors told Mrs. Zerbe that Greve had saved Dean's life.

Greve and his wife have two small children and have lived near the Zerbe family for only two weeks.

We must refuse to compromise with expediency. We must maintain the courage to defy the consensus. We must continue to choose the harder right instead of the easier wrong.

It has been said that history turns on small hinges, and so do people's lives. We are constantly making small decisions, some of them apparently trivial. The total of these decisions finally determines the success or failure of our lives.

That is why it is worthwhile to look ahead, to set a course, and so to be at least partly ready when the moment of decision comes. By anticipating events we avoid muddle-headedness.

Royal Bank of Canada Newsletter

One of the imperative requirements of life is to be able to make choices. In order to do so, one must know how to look at things and oneself. One must also learn that to live means being able to cope with difficulties. Problems are a normal part of life, and the great thing is to avoid being flattened by them. One has to grapple, instead of diving for the cyclone shelter every time a strong wind blows.

Royal Bank of Canada Newsletter

145

Courage becomes a living and attractive virtue when it is regarded not as willingness to die manfully, but as the determination to live decently. A moral coward is one who is afraid to do what he thinks is right because other men will disapprove or laugh.

Royal Bank of Canada Newsletter

It must not be expected that the road of life spreads itself in an unobstructed view before the person starting his journey. He must anticipate coming upon forks and turnings in the road. But he cannot hope to reach his desired journey's end if he thinks aimlessly about whether to go East or West. He must make decisions purposefully.

Royal Bank of Canada Newsletter

All great leaders have deliberated with caution but acted with decision and promptness.

All men have fears, but those who face their fears with dignity have courage as well.

Ernest Hemingway

Courage does not consist in refusing to admit danger when the danger is there. Courage avoids taking foolhardy or frivolous risks. Courage is strength of mind that gives you the physical strength to act. Courage is the self-esteem that gives you the urge to undertake a job without waiting for others who might bear part of the blame for failure.

Royal Bank of Canada Newsletter

Preparation for Achievement

You see things and you say, "Why?" But I dream things that never were, and I say, "Why not?"

George Bernard Shaw

Never, never, never, never give in.

Sir Winston Churchill

June 6, 1973, LOS ANGELES (UPI) — A blind father rescued his three year old daughter from drowning Tuesday, finding her under water in a swimming pool by tracking the sound of air bubbles from her lungs.

Thomas Sullivan, 26, told police his daughter Blythe fell in the pool at the family home while he was on the telephone. He heard the splash, he said, and ran outside. Standing beside the pool, he listened to the sound of air bubbles rising to the surface and moved about the pool until he thought he had the source located, then jumped in and found the girl under seven feet of water.

Blythe was revived by mouth-to-mouth resuscitation and was reported in satisfactory condition.

Do it! Do it right! Do it right now!

Eagles see rivers but fly over them; wise men meet obstacles but overcome them.

William Arthur Ward

The critical step in handling any challenging occurrence is making the decision about what to do. No one can be successful in business or private life unless he is able to make decisions backed by resolution. The important thing is to do what your good judgment tells you offers some probability of success, even though you know that if you were given time to think and to plan, you might come up with a better scheme.

Royal Bank of Canada Newsletter

The fine art of executive decision consists in not deciding questions that are not now pertinent, in not deciding prematurely, in not making decisions that cannot be made effective, and in not making decisions that others should make.

Chester I. Barnard

The unconditional surrender of our enemies was a signal for the greatest outburst of joy in the history of mankind. The Second World War had indeed been fought to the bitter end in Europe. The vanquished as well as the victors felt inexpressable relief. But for us in Britain and the British Empire, who had alone been in the struggle from the first day to the last and staked our existence on the result, there was meaning behind what even our most powerful and most valiant allies could feel. Weary and worn, impoverished but undaunted and now triumphant, we had a moment that was sublime. We gave thanks to God for the noblest of all His blessings: the sense we had done our duty.

Sir Winston Churchill

148

Preparation for Achievement

―――――――――――◆―――――――――――

Let us have faith that right makes might, and in that faith let us to the end, dare to do our duty as we understand it.

Abraham Lincoln

―――――――――――◆―――――――――――

It isn't enough to do one's best. One must do what is necessary.

Sir Winston Churchill

―――――――――――◆―――――――――――

Life is a sea upon which the proud are humbled, the shirker exposed and the leader revealed. To sail it safely and reach your desired port, you need to keep your charts at hand and up to date. You need to learn by the experience of others to stand firm for principles, to broaden your interests, to be understanding of the rights of others to sail the same sea, and to be reliable in your discharge of duty.

Royal Bank of Canada Newsletter

―――――――――――◆―――――――――――

LEND A HAND

I am only one, but I am one;
I can't do everything, but I can do something.
What I can do, that I ought to do;
What I ought to do,
By the grace of God I will do!

Edward Everett Hale

―――――――――――◆―――――――――――

I know what pleasure is, for I have done good work.

Robert Louis Stevenson

―――――――――――◆―――――――――――

Bill Brown made a million — Bill Brown! Think of that!
A boy, you remember, as poor as a rat;
He hoed for the neighbors, did jobs by the day,
But Bill made a million, or near it, they say.
You can't understand it? Well, neither could I,
And then I remembered, and now I know why:
The bell might be ringing, the dinner horn blow,
But Bill always hoed to the end of the row.

Bill worked for my father, you maybe recall;
He wasn't a wonder — not that, not at all;
He couldn't out-hoe me, or cover more ground,
Or hoe any cleaner, or beat me around.
In fact, I was better in one way that I know:
One toot from the kitchen and home I would go;
But Bill always hoed to the end of the row.

We used to get hungry out there in the corn.
When you talk about music, what equals a horn?
A horn yellin' dinner, tomatoes and beans,
And pork and potatoes and gravy and greens?
I ain't blamin' no one for quittin' on time,
To stop with the whistle, that ain't a crime.
But as for the million — well, this much I know:
That Bill always hoed to the end of the row.

When I do good, I feel good; and when I do bad, I feel bad.

Abraham Lincoln

"He that findeth his life shall lose it: and he that loseth his
life for my sake shall find it."

Matthew 10:39

Preparation for Achievement

—————————◆—————————

Having started moving in the right direction, a youth needs to realize an ancient but still valid truth: that nothing can be had for nothing. If a man wishes to reach the top of a hill, he must not shirk the trouble of climbing. He may fail, and failure has a certain dignity—but not failure to try.

—————————◆—————————

Brightly beams our Father's mercy from His lighthouse
  evermore,
But to us He gives the keeping of the lights along the shore.
Dark the night of sin has settled: Lord, the angry billows
  roar.
Eager eyes are watching, longing; for the lights along
  the shore.
Trim your feeble lamp, my brother; some poor sailor
  tempest-tossed,
Trying now to make the harbor, in the darkness may be lost.
Let the lower lights be burning; send a gleam across the
  wave;
Some poor fainting, struggling seaman you may rescue,
  you may save.

Phillip Paul Bliss

—————————◆—————————

It was said of Abraham Lincoln: "He prayed as if everything depended upon God, and he worked as if everything depended upon himself."

—————————◆—————————

We are such stuff as dreams are made on.

William Shakespeare

—————————◆—————————

---◆---

"Do all things without murmurings and disputings: that ye may be blameless and harmless, the sons of God, without rebuke, in the midst of a crooked and perverse nation, among whom ye shine as lights in the world."

Philippians 2:14,15

---◆---

When an administrator in Africa rode out to inspect land that had been devastated by a storm, he came to a place where giant cedars had been uprooted and destroyed. He said to his official in charge of forestry, "You will have to plant some cedars here."

The official replied, "It takes two thousand years to grow cedars the size these were. They don't even bear cones until they are fifty years old."

"Then," said the administrator, "we must plant them at once!"

Royal Bank of Canada Newsletter

---◆---

Nothing great was ever achieved without enthusiasm.

Ralph Waldo Emerson

---◆---

Enthusiasm is the genius of sincerity, and truth accomplishes no victories without it.

Edward Bulwer-Lytton

---◆---

There is one thing more contagious than enthusiasm, and that is the lack of enthusiasm.

---◆---

Preparation for Achievement

———————————◆———————————

On October 6, 1955, a United Airlines plane crashed into the top of Medicine Box Mountain in Wyoming. Sixty-five people lost their lives. The pilot was flying at 12,000 feet. If he had been flying at 12,055 feet, the greatest air disaster in American history to that date could have been averted, and the lives of sixty-five people would have been saved. What a difference a few more feet in altitude would have made to those people and their families. Even though the plane was exerting the power and thrust it needed, and everything was riding smoothly, just one little mistake made a big difference.

Let us take an example from this accident and make sure we make it over the last few feet. Don't let it be said that we were riding smoothly and then all of a sudden found that we had not put forth enough effort to get us over the top—and ended in failure.

———————————◆———————————

Genius is: (1) the power to visualize the objective; (2) constancy of purpose; and (3) ability to make continuous effort.

———————————◆———————————

After all that has been said, the greatest and most important duty is to preach the Gospel.

Joseph Smith

———————————◆———————————

"Fear God, and keep his commandments: for this is the whole duty of man."

Ecclesiastes 12:13

———————————◆———————————

Preparation for Achievement

————————————◆————————————

You can buy a man's time; you can buy a man's physical presence at a given time and place; you can even buy a measured number of skilled muscular motions per hour or day; but you cannot buy enthusiasm. You cannot buy devotion of hearts, minds, and souls. You have to earn these things.

Clarence Frances

————————————◆————————————

What does it mean to magnify a calling? It means to build it up in dignity and importance, to make it honorable and commendable in the eyes of all men, to enlarge and strengthen it, to let the light of heaven shine through it to the view of other men. And how does one magnify a calling? Simply by performing the service that pertains to it. An Elder magnifies the ordained calling of an Elder by learning what his duties as an Elder are and then by doing them.

————————————◆————————————

The fight song of Yonkers High School in New York contains a verse: "Lead us, oh lead us, Great Molder of Men, out of the darkness to strive once again."

————————————◆————————————

If we don't try, we don't do; and if we don't do, then why are we here?

Shenandoah

————————————◆————————————

The poorest man is not one who does not have a cent but one who does not have a dream.

————————————◆————————————

154

Preparation for Achievement

These are the times that try men's souls. The summer soldier and the sunshine patriot will, in this crisis, shrink from the service of his country; but he that stands it *now,* deserves the love and thanks of man and woman. Tyranny, like hell, is not easily conquered; yet we have this consolation with us, that the harder the conflict, the more glorious the triumph.

Thomas Paine

If you do not magnify your calling, God will hold you responsible for those you might have saved had you done your duty.

John Taylor

If a person is to walk with head held high, he must make his contribution to life. If he is to fulfill his destiny, he must leave the world a little richer and better than it would have been had he not lived and performed his services.

Royal Bank of Canada Newsletter

DUTY

I slept and dreamed that life was Beauty:
I woke and found that life was Duty:
Was then thy dream a shadowy lie?
Toil on, sad heart, courageously,
And thou shalt find thy dream to be
A noonday light and truth to thee.

Ellen S. Hooper

155

Preparation for Achievement

———————————◆———————————

The heights by great men reached and kept
Were not attained by sudden flight,
But they, while their companions slept,
Were toiling upward in the night.

Henry Wadsworth Longfellow

———————————◆———————————

THE CHAMPION

The average runner sprints
Until the breath in him is gone;
But the champion has the iron will;
That makes him carry on.

For rest, the average runner begs,
When limp his muscles grow;
But the champion runs on leaden legs
His spirit makes him go.

The average man's complacent
When he does his best to score;
But the champion does his best
And then he does a little more.

———————————◆———————————

The most realistic self-image of all is to conceive of yourself
as made in the image of God. You cannot sincerely hold
this conviction without experiencing a profound new sense
of strength and power.

Maxwell Maltz

———————————◆———————————

You can't be right by doing wrong, and you can't be wrong
by doing right.

Thomas S. Monson

———————————◆———————————

Preparation for Achievement

———————————◆———————————

There comes a day when the worrisome checkbook, the jangling telephone, the brainstorming conference, the pressures of being a man in the jet age, have to be set aside.

There even comes a day when he just can't take his daughter's hockey stick or wrestle with his son's algebra. It's time for him to be alone, to think things through, to put the "Out to lunch" sign on his heart and nervous system.

Time to go fishing.

Time to sit in the sun.

He'll assume his role as a better husband, a better father, a better friend, a better worker, if he's urged to be alone once in a while, out of the intense glare of a demanding man-made turmoil and into the tranquil world of nature.

Royal Bank of Canada Newsletter

———————————◆———————————

Stick to your task 'til it sticks to you;
Beginners are many, but enders are few.
Honor, power, place and praise
Will come, in time, to the one who stays.

Stick to your task 'til it sticks to you;
Bend at it, sweat at it, smile at it too;
For out of the bend and the sweat and the smile
Will come life's victories, after awhile.

———————————◆———————————

If a thing is right, it can be done; if wrong, it can be done without.

———————————◆———————————

If you think you might fail, you tend not to try.

———————————◆———————————

◆

For workers in World War II with ties to the men on the battlefronts — the fathers, mothers, brothers, sisters, and wives on the production lines at home — there was a special incentive that outweighed everything else: the possibility that their own handiwork might somehow directly affect the life of a loved one. They relished the story of a seaman named Elgin Staples, whose ship went down off Guadalcanal. Staples was swept over the side; but he survived, thanks to a life belt that proved, on later examination, to have been inspected, packed, and stamped back home in Akron, Ohio, by his own mother.

Ronald H. Bailey

◆

At Westminster Abbey, on the plaque beneath which lies the Unknown Soldier, is this inscription: "They buried him among the kings because he had done good toward God and toward his house."

◆

Nurture your mind with great thoughts, for you will never go any higher than you think.

Benjamin Disraeli

◆

I find the great thing in this world is not so much where we stand, as in what direction we are moving: To reach the port of heaven, we must sail sometimes with the wind and sometimes against it — but we must sail, and not drift, nor lie at anchor.

Oliver Wendell Holmes

◆

Preparation for Achievement

◆

After the big London fire in 1066, the great English architect, Sir Christopher Wren, volunteered his services to plan and superintend the building of one of the world's greatest cathedrals. Unknown to most of the workmen, he passed among them often, watching the construction. To three stone cutters one day he put the same question: "What are you doing?"

One of them answered, "I am cutting this stone."

Another answered, "I am earning my three shillings per day."

But the third stood up, squared his shoulders and proudly said, "I am helping Sir Christopher Wren build this magnificent cathedral."

The Scouter's Minute

◆

When Elder John A. Widtsoe was made a member of the Council of the Twelve, he was president of the University of Utah. A professor in the East wrote to him and said: "I do not understand why you should resign as president of a great state university to become affiliated with any Church organization."

Elder Widtsoe's reply was, in part: "I am only as clay in the hands of the Potter, for my time is mine only to serve with, and it matters little to me in what capacity I am asked to spend my time and strength."

◆

Under a cartoon depicting the log cabin which was Abraham Lincoln's home, we read: "Lincoln: ill-housed, ill-fed, ill-clothed."

◆

◆

Duty is the sublimest word in our language. Do your duty in all things. You cannot do more. You should never wish to do less.

Robert Edward Lee

◆

TRUE NOBILITY

Who does his task from day to day
And meets whatever comes his way,
Believing God has willed it so,
Has found real greatness here below.

Who guards his post, no matter where,
Believing God must need him there,
Although but lowly toil it be,
Has risen to nobility.

For great and low there's but one test;
'Tis that each man shall do his best.
Who works with all the strength he can
Shall never die in debt to man.

Edgar A. Guest

◆

Enthusiasm is interest plus energy. People are defeated in life not because of want of ability, but for lack of whole-hearted effort.

Royal Bank of Canada Newsletter

◆

One cannot rest content with mediocrity when excellence is within his grasp.

Thomas S. Monson

◆

Preparation for Achievement

One must have the adventurous daring to accept oneself as a bundle of possibilities and undertake the most interesting game in the world: making the most of one's best.

Harry Emerson Fosdick

Every job is a self-portrait of the person who did it. Autograph your work with excellence.

When Wilma Rudolph was a little girl in Tennessee, she had to walk with braces, her legs weakened with polio, double pneumonia, and scarlet fever.

At nineteen she became the first American woman to win three gold medals in a single Olympiad, setting world records in three events along the way.

She attributed her successes to determination, faith, and hard work which enabled her to rise above her childhood handicaps and become a world-class athlete.

Tom McCarthey

Our responsibility is to lengthen our stride.

Spencer W. Kimball

A lesson in persistence was given in the log of Columbus's first voyage across the uncharted Atlantic. Day after day he wrote: "This day we sailed on."

---◆---

If one were to enumerate the marks of greatness which characterize those who achieve, perhaps prominent mention would be made of faith, of prayer, testimony, effort, constancy of purpose, or ability to plan or to be obedient to self-discipline. All of these are indeed marks of greatness which will contribute to the success of anyone.

However, there is an additional mark which underlies the attitude and the life of great men. I have rarely, if ever, seen a leader who did not possess it. This mark of greatness is a willingness to give of oneself. The Lord himself declared, "Behold, the Lord requireth the heart and a willing mind; and the willing and obedient shall eat of the good of the land of Zion in these last days." (D&C 64:34.)

We read in the Book of Mormon that, before candidates were baptized, they expressed a willingness to bear one another's burdens.

Our Savior willingly died, that all men might live again. Are we ready to live willingly and serve willingly? If so, one of the marks of greatness will have been achieved in our lives.

Thomas S. Monson

---◆---

Inscription on the wall of the Library of Congress: "The history of the world is the biography of great men."

---◆---

There's a prison warden who makes a speech to prisoners and young people entitled "Thirty Seconds That Can Save Your Life." He stresses the importance of waiting just thirty seconds to think over a rash act before doing it. The same speech could apply to thinking over what we're going to say.

---◆---

Preparation for Achievement

When the secretary of President George Washington tried to excuse his lateness by saying his watch was slow, Washington replied, "Then you must get a new watch or I another secretary." Isn't it quite likely that God may feel the same way about us when we continously and habitually violate this first law of order, which is punctuality?

Sterling W. Sill

Build thee more stately mansions, O my soul,
As the swift seasons roll!
Leave thy low-vaulted past!
Let each new temple, nobler than the last,
Shut thee from heaven with a dome more vast,
Till thou at length art free,
Leaving thine outgrown shell by life's unresting sea!

Oliver Wendell Holmes

Ideals are like stars: You will not succeed in touching them with your hands, but like the seafaring man on the desert of waters, you choose them as your guides, and following them you will reach your destination.

Carl Schurz

"When we take people," thou wouldst say, "merely as they are, we make them worse; when we treat them as if they were what they should be, we improve them as far as they can be improved."

Johann Wolfgang von Goethe

---◆---

Sometimes the hardest thing in life is simply to put one foot in front of the other — to keep going. And, sometimes, the most worthwhile things in life are accomplished inch by inch, by people who are struggling not for greatness but simply to put one foot in front of the other. Seldom has this been more clearly illustrated than in an incident in the career of Walter Johnson, one of the greatest pitchers in the history of baseball. Johnson was scheduled to pitch a crucial game, but his arm was painfully sore that day. His manager, Clark Griffith, told him, "Try one inning. If your arm gives you trouble, I'll take you out." After an inning, Johnson's arm still pained him, but he said he would try another. He pitched the second and then the third. At the conclusion of nine innings of out-and-out agony, he had pitched the *only* no-hitter in his twenty-year career.

---◆---

Nothing in the world can take the place of persistence. Talent will not; nothing is more common than unsuccessful men with talent. Genius will not; unrewarded it's almost a proverb. Education will not; the world is filled with educated derelicts. Persistence and determination alone are onmipotent.

Calvin Coolidge

---◆---

Almost everything that is great has been done by youth.

Benjamin Disraeli

---◆---

That which stirs the pulses of youth are the love of knowledge and the joy of the discovery of the causes of things.

Aldous Huxley

---◆---

164

Preparation for Achievement

◆

Tolstoy wrote: "There never has been and cannot be a good life without self-control." More recently, Lord Beaverbook said that a man "can only keep his judgment intact, his nerves sound and his mind secure by the process of self-discipline."

Royal Bank of Canada Newsletter

◆

IF —

If you can talk with crowds and keep your virtue,
Or walk with kings — nor lose the common touch;
If neither foes nor loving friends can hurt you;
If all men count with you, but none too much;
If you can fill the unforgiving minute
With sixty seconds' worth of distance run —
Yours is the Earth and everything that's in it,
And — which is more — you'll be a Man, my son!

Rudyard Kipling

◆

The virtue of all achievement is victory over oneself. Those who know this victory can never know defeat.

A. J. Cronin

◆

Live fish swim upstream.

◆

My experiments never came about by chance. I *worked!*

Thomas A. Edison

◆

TEN STEPS TO SUCCESS

1. Find your own particular talent.
2. Be big in all you do.
3. Be honest.
4. Live with enthusiasm.
5. Don't let your possessions possess you.
6. Don't worry.
7. Look up to people when you can; look down on no one.
8. Don't cling to the past.
9. Assume your full share of responsibility in the world.
10. Pray consistently.

A man's personal philosophy, his way of looking at the world and the men and women around him, determine his success as a manager of things and people more than any other single factor. His basic attitudes are far more significant than the techniques he uses. The executive's skill with people — or lack of it — is the determining element in his long-range success or failure.

Stanley F. Teele

Success is the progressive realization of a worthy ideal.

It has been said of a man who seized his opportunities with success that he "stumbled on a good idea." There may be some truth in the comment, but the whole truth is that the moment of inspiration would not have come to him if he had not prepared himself for it. Pasteur once wrote that "chance favours only the prepared mind."

Preparation for Achievement

Each man has his own vocation. The talent is the call. There is one direction in which all space is open to him. He has faculties silently inviting him thither to endless exertion. He is like a ship in a river; he runs against obstructions on every side but one. On that side all obstruction is taken away, and he sweeps serenely over a deepening channel into an infinite sea.

Ralph Waldo Emerson

If a man has a talent and cannot use it, he has failed. If he has a talent and uses only half of it, he has partly failed. If he has a talent and learns somehow to use the whole of it, he has gloriously succeeded, and won a satisfaction and a triumph few men ever know.

Thomas Wolfe

The woods would be very silent if no birds sang there except those who sang best.

John James Audubon

Great men have not been merely dreamers. They have returned from their visions to the practicalities of replacing the airy stones of their dream castles with solid masonry wrought by their hands.

Initiative is doing the right thing at the right time without having to be told.

―――――――――◆―――――――――

Sloth is one of the seven deadly sins, responsible for a great deal of the failing and underachieving we see; but idling away one's time is not enjoying life. "Not to be occupied and not to exist amount to the same thing," said Voltaire. And Emerson followed up with: "God offers to every mind its choice between truth and repose. Take what you please; you can never have both."

―――――――――◆―――――――――

You can't legislate equality; you have to deserve it. You can't demand success; you have to earn it. You can't be handed an education or skill; you have to learn by hard work. You can't vote yourself security; you have to produce for it and save for it. For hundreds of years false leaders have preached, "Give me your support and I will care for you. I will take from others and give you a living you don't have to work for." And for those same hundreds of years men have been drugging themselves into that dream—and waking up, not in Heaven, but in Purgatory.

KSL Editorial
Salt Lake City, Utah

―――――――――◆―――――――――

"He that gathereth in summer is a wise son: but he that sleepeth in harvest is a son that causeth shame."

Proverbs 10:5

―――――――――◆―――――――――

It is better to light one small candle than to curse the darkness.

Confucius

―――――――――◆―――――――――

168

Preparation for Achievement

———◆———

STORMS BRING OUT THE EAGLES
BUT THE LITTLE BIRDS TAKE COVER

When the "storms of life" gather darkly ahead,
I think of these wonderful words I once read
And I say to myself as "threatening clouds" hover
Don't "fold up your wings" and "run for cover"
But like the eagle "spread wide your wings"
and "soar far above" the trouble life brings,
For the eagle knows that the higher he flies
The more tranquil and brighter become the skies . . .
And there is nothing in life God ever asks us to bear
That we can't soar above "On the Wings of Prayer,"
And in looking back over the "storm you passed through"
You'll find you gained strength and new courage, too,
For in facing "life's storms" with an eagle's wings
You can fly far above earth's small, petty things.

Helen Steiner Rice

———◆———

Wherefore, when we build let us think that we build
forever. Let it not be for present delight, nor for present
use alone; let it be such work as our descendants will thank
us for, and let us think as we lay stone on stone that a time
is to come when those stones will be held sacred, because
our hands have touched them; and men will say, as they
look upon the labour and wrought substances of them:
"See, this our fathers did for us."

John Ruskin

———◆———

Inscription on the wall of the Library of Congress: "Too
low they build who build beneath the stars."

———◆———

169

THE BRIDGE BUILDER

An old man going a lone highway
Came at the evening, cold and gray,
To a chasm, vast and wide and steep,
With waters rolling cold and deep.
The old man crossed in the twilight dim,
That sullen stream had no fears for him;
But he turned when safe on the other side,
And built a bridge to span the tide.

"Old man," said a fellow pilgrim near,
"You are wasting your strength with building here.
Your journey will end with the ending day,
You never again will pass this way.
You've crossed the chasm, deep and wide,
Why build you this bridge at eventide?"

The builder lifted his old gray head.
"Good friend, in the path I have come," he said,
"There followeth after me today
A youth whose feet must pass this way.
This chasm that has been naught to me
To that fair-haired youth may a pitfall be.
He, too, must cross in the twilight dim —
Good friend, I am building the bridge for him."

William Allen Dromgoole

There is no greater nor more satisfying reward than
that which comes from discovering and developing men.
The possibilities are almost unlimited. Talent, like oil, is
discovered in unexpected places and in surprising
quantities.

A. A. Stambaugh

Preparation for Achievement

A new hospital administrator, holding his first staff meeting, thought that a rather difficult matter had been settled to everyone's satisfaction when one of the participants suddenly asked, "Would this have satisfied Nurse Bryan?" At once the argument started all over and did not subside until a new and much more ambitious solution to the problem had been hammered out.

Nurse Bryan, the administrator learned, had been a long-serving nurse at the hospital. She was not particularly distinguished, had not in fact ever been a supervisor. But whenever a decision on patient care came up on her floor, Nurse Bryan would ask, "Are we doing the best we can do to help this patient?" Patients on Nurse Bryan's floor did better and recovered faster. Gradually over the years, the whole hospital had learned to adopt what came to be known as "Nurse Bryan's rule." They had learned to ask: "Are we really making the best contribution to the purpose of this hospital?"

Though Nurse Bryan herself had retired almost ten years earlier, the standards she had set still made demands on people who, in terms of training and position, were her superiors.

Commitment to contribution is commitment to responsible effectiveness. Without it, a man shortchanges himself, deprives his organization, and cheats the people with whom he works.

Peter Drucker

Leisure without study is death; it is a tomb for the living man.

Lucius Annaeus Seneca

171

Leaders of the Church, then, should be men not easily discouraged, not without hope, and not given to forebodings of all sorts of evils to come. . . . If men standing in high places sometimes feel the weight and anxiety of a momentous time, they should be all the firmer and all the more resolute in those convictions which come from a God-fearing conscience and pure lives. . . . It is a matter of the greatest importance that the people be educated to appreciate and cultivate the bright side of life rather than to permit its darkness and shadows to hover over them.

Joseph F. Smith

The world has not a man who is an idler in his own eyes.

Far better it is to dare mighty things, to win glorious triumphs, even though checkered by failure, than to take rank with those poor spirits who neither enjoy much nor suffer much, because they live in the gray twilight that knows not victory nor defeat.

Theodore Roosevelt

No one is proud of what he intends to do.

Henry Ford

Inspiration is a guest who does not visit the lazy or the procrastinator as often as he does the busy and diligent.

Preparation for Achievement

There is a quotation which serves as the foreword to the first book of *Northwest Passage*, a novel of exploration and adventure during the latter half of the eighteenth century. It fittingly reflects the theme and subject matter of the book as a whole. The book is the story of two men. . . . Both men exhibit the unextinguishable spark that compels them onward — one toward the realization of a dream, the other toward the fulfillment of a talent. The quotation follows: "On every side of us are men who hunt perpetually for their personal Northwest Passage, too often sacrificing health, strength and life itself to the search; and who shall say they are not happier in their vain but hopeful quest than wiser, duller folk who sit at home, venturing nothing."

Kenneth Rogers

You say you love me, but sometimes you don't show it. In the beginning you couldn't do enough for me. Now you seem to take me for granted. Some days I even wonder if I mean anything at all to you.

Maybe when I'm gone you'll appreciate me and all the things I do for you. I'm responsible for getting food on your table, for your clean shirt, for the welfare of your children . . . a thousand and one things you want and need. Why, if it weren't for me, you wouldn't even have a car. I've kept quiet and waited to see how long it would take for you to realize how much you really need me.

Cherish me, take care of me and I'll continue to take good care of you. Who am I? I am your job.

Tool and Die Institute
News Bulletin

QUESTION NOT

Question not, but live and labor,
Till your goal be won,
Helping every feeble neighbor,
Seeking help from none;
Life is mostly froth and bubble,
Two things stand like stone —
Kindness in another's trouble,
Courage in our own.

Adam Lindsay Gordon

TEN RULES OF HAPPINESS

1. Develop yourself by self-discipline.
2. Joy comes through creation, sorrow through destruction.
3. Do things which are hard to do.
4. Entertain uplifting thoughts.
5. Do your best this hour, and you will do better the next.
6. Be true to those who trust you.
7. Pray for wisdom, courage, and a kind heart.
8. Give heed to God's messages.
9. True friends enrich life; if you would have friends, be one.
10. Faith is the foundation of all things, including happiness.

David O. McKay

If you do not think about the future, you cannot have one.

John Galsworthy

———————◆———————

Decision is of little account unless it is followed by action, and there is no recipe as good for getting things done as the one to start doing them.

———————◆———————

The only person who ever got his work done by Friday was Robinson Crusoe.

A. J. Marshall

———————◆———————

It has been said that industry is a better horse to ride than genius.

———————◆———————

Think of your objectives, not your obstacles. Don't try to find excuses for your failures.

N. Eldon Tanner

———————◆———————

We have forty million reasons for failure, but not a single excuse.

———————◆———————

In *The King and I*, by Rodgers and Hammerstein, the following conversation takes place between Anna and her son, Louis:

"Was he as good a king as he could have been?" Louis asked.

"Louis, I don't think any man has ever been as good a King as he could have been; but this one tried — he tried very hard."

———————◆———————

IT COULDN'T BE DONE

Somebody said that it couldn't be done,
But he with a chuckle replied
That "maybe it couldn't," but he would be one
Who wouldn't say so till he'd tried.
So he buckled right in with the trace of a grin
On his face. If he worried he hid it.
He started to sing as he tackled the thing
That couldn't be done, and he did it.

Somebody scoffed: "Oh, you'll never do that;
At least no one ever has done it";
But he took off his coat and he took off his hat,
And the first thing we knew he'd begun it.
With a lift of his chin and a bit of a grin,
Without any doubting or quiddit,
He started to sing as he tackled the thing
That couldn't be done, and he did it!

There are thousands to tell you it cannot be done.
There are thousands to prophesy failure;
There are thousands to point out to you, one by one,
The dangers that wait to assail you.
But just buckle in with a bit of a grin,
Just take off your coat and go to it;
Just start to sing as you tackle the thing
That "cannot be done," and you'll do it.

Edgar A. Guest

The difference between what we call a good man and a bad man may not be so much the impulses they have as how they control them.

Preparation for Achievement

―――――――――――――◆―――――――――――――

I THINK CONTINUALLY OF THOSE

I think continually of those who were truly great—
The names of those who in their lives fought for life,
Who wore at their hearts the fire's center.
Born of the sun they traveled a short while toward the sun,
And left the vivid air signed with their honor.

Stephen Spender

―――――――――――――◆―――――――――――――

The Lord doesn't ask about our inabilities or abilities. He
only asks about our availabilities. If we show our dependa-
bility, He will help us in our capability.

Neal A. Maxwell

―――――――――――――◆―――――――――――――

It's the steady, constant driving
To the goal for which you're striving,
Not the speed with which you travel
That will make the victory sure.
It's the everlasting gaining,
Without whimper or complaining
At the burdens you are bearing,
Or the woes you must endure.

It's the holding to a purpose
And the never giving in;
It's the cutting down the distance
By the little that you win.
It's the iron will to do it
And the steady sticking to it.
So, whate'er your task, go to it
And life's purpose you will win.

―――――――――――――◆―――――――――――――

Preparation for Achievement

———————————◆———————————

It is practically a law in life that when one door closes to us, another opens. The trouble is that we often look with so much regret and longing upon the closed door that we do not see the one which has opened to us. We no doubt see challenges and problems before us. Let us see, with equal clarity, the promises.

———————————◆———————————

Only a mediocre person is always at his best.

Somerset Maugham

———————————◆———————————

Before you can move anyone else, you must move yourself.

Socrates

———————————◆———————————

You can become strongest at your weakest place.

John Mott

———————————◆———————————

The journey of a thousand miles begins with one step.

Laotse

———————————◆———————————

Every person is in reality two persons: He is the person he is today, and he is the person he could become tomorrow and in the future.

———————————◆———————————

Preparation for Achievement

The greatest achievement of the human spirit is to live up to one's opportunities and make the most of one's resources.

"Four things come not back:" says an Arabian proverb, "the spoken word, the spent arrow, the past life and the neglected opportunity." It is easy to let life slide by, as children at the seashore fill their hands with sand and let the grains flow through their fingers until all are gone; but it is mentally unhealthy for mature people to let opportunities slip away like that.

Nothing ever does itself. Nothing ever memorizes itself. Nothing ever accomplishes itself without the requisite effort. Carlyle said: "Men do less than they ought, unless they do all that they can." It is not enough just to try; we have to succeed. The Lord expects us to see things through.

I do not ask for any crown
But that which all may win;
Nor try to conquer any world
Except the one within.

Louisa May Alcott

No honors are too distant for the man who prepares himself with patience.

Patriotism
and
Holidays

Patriotism
and
Holidays

So many signs of Christmas!
We see them everywhere.
There's such a strange excitement;
We feel it in the air.

So many friends at Christmas!
With you we'd like to share
This lovely, strange excitement,
Because we know you care.

Primary Children's Hospital
Christmas Card

My door is on the latch to-night,
The hearth fire is aglow.
I seem to hear swift passing feet,
The Christ Child in the snow.

My heart is open wide to-night
For stranger, kith or kin.
I would not bar a single door
Where Love might enter in!

Kate Douglas Wiggin

THE THREE KINGS

Three Kings came riding from far away:
Melchior and Gaspar and Balthazar.
Three Wise Men out of the East were they,
And they travelled by night and they slept by day;
For their guide was a beautiful, wonderful star.

Henry Wadsworth Longfellow

I sometimes think we expect too much of Christmas day.
We try to crowd into it the long arrears of kindliness and
humanity of the whole year.

David Grayson

A FRIEND'S GREETING

I'd like to be the sort of friend that you have been to me;
I'd like to be the help that you've been always glad to be;
I'd like to mean as much to you each minute of the day
As you have meant, good friend of mine, to me along
   the way.

I'm wishing at this Christmas time that I could but repay
A portion of the gladness that you've strewn along my way;
And could I have one wish this year, this only would it be:
I'd like to be the sort of friend that you have been to me.

Edgar A. Guest

Christmas is the family time, the good time of year.

Samuel Johnson

Despite discouragement and disheartening conditions throughout the world, Christmas is the happiest season of the whole year. But let us ever keep in mind that people are most blessed whose daily conduct most nearly comports with the teachings and example of Jesus Christ our Lord and Savior, at whose birth was proclaimed: "Peace on earth, good will toward men."

David O. McKay

Christmas is sharing of joys, memories, homes, and thoughts. A sharing of what we have — with our loved ones and with those who are less fortunate.

Christmas is a sharing of emotions; a sharing of our hopes and dreams for the year to come; a sharing of food, conversation, and laughter.

Christmas is a sharing of the beauty and wonder of the little Child who has inspired millions of lives since that night when angels sang: "Glory to God in the highest!"

Pearl S. Buck

Keeping Christmas is good, but sharing it is better.

Arnold Glasow

I will honor Christmas in my heart and try to keep it all the year. I will live in the Past, the Present and the Future. The spirits of all three shall strive within me. I will not shut out the lessons that they teach.

Charles Dickens

The best Christmas gift of all is the presence of a happy family all wrapped up in each other.

Woodmen of the World Magazine

"Lift up your head and be of good cheer; for behold, the time is at hand, and on this night shall the sign be given, and on the morrow come I into the world, to show unto the world that I will fulfill all that which I have caused to be spoken by the mouth of my holy prophets."

3 Nephi 1:13

I HEARD THE BELLS ON CHRISTMAS DAY

Then pealed the bells more loud and deep:
"God is not dead, nor doth he sleep;
The wrong shall fail, the right prevail,
With peace on earth, good will to men."

Henry Wadsworth Longfellow

Rings and jewels are not gifts, but apologies for gifts. The only true gift is a portion of thyself.

Ralph Waldo Emerson

"For unto us a child is born . . . and his name shall be called . . . The Prince of Peace."

Isaiah 9:6

Where charity stands watching and faith holds wide the door the dark night wakes—the glory breaks, and Christmas comes once more.

Phillips Brooks

A BIRTHDAY GIFT

What can I give Him,
Poor as I am?
If I were a shepherd
I would bring a lamb,
If I were a Wise Man
I would do my part,
Yet what can I give Him,
Give my heart.

Christina Rossetti

CHRISTMAS 1847

On that Christmas, in this valley stood
Rude homes of men around the Old Fort Square.
Two thousand souls or less were living there,
Bound by the ties of faith and brotherhood.
All day they labored—some with hammer's din,
Some molding 'dobe bricks, mud to their knees.
Thankful the dreaded winter still was mild;
They sang, with happy wives and babes within
A shelter mean, as cradled Mary's child.
But unlike us, in surfeit hard to please,
In each brave heart there was a Yuletide glow
Of gratitude that we can never know.

Jessie Miller Robinson

187

THE CHRISTMAS SPIRIT

I am the Christmas Spirit.

I enter the home of poverty, causing pale-faced children to open their eyes wide in pleased wonder.

I cause the miser's clutched hand to relax, and thus paint a bright spot on his soul.

I cause the aged to renew their youth and to laugh in the glad old way.

I keep romance alive in the heart of childhood, and brighten sleep with dreams woven of magic.

I cause eager feet to climb dark stairways with filled baskets, leaving behind hearts amazed at the goodness of the world.

I cause the prodigal to pause a moment on his wild, wasteful way, and send to anxious love some little token that releases glad tears — tears which wash away the hard lines of sorrow.

I enter dark prison cells, reminding scarred manhood of what might have been, and pointing forward to good days yet to come.

I come softly into the still, white home of pain, and lips that are too weak to speak just tremble in silent, eloquent gratitude.

In a thousand ways I cause the weary world to look up into the face of God and for a little moment forget the things that are small and wretched.

I am the Christmas Spirit.

Unknown

"And the angel said unto them, Fear not: for behold, I bring you good tidings of great joy, which shall be to all people. For unto you is born this day in the city of David a Saviour, which is Christ the Lord."

Luke 2:10-11

From the diary of Mrs. Rebecca Riter, December 25, 1847, Great Salt Lake Valley: "The winter was cold. Christmas came and the children were hungry. I had brought a peck of wheat across the plains and hid it under a pile of wood. I thought I would cook a handful of wheat for the baby. Then I thought how we would need wheat for seed in the spring, so I left it alone."

Christmas — a Christmas of comfort and joy, of love among those who are with their families, of soft memories among those who are enduring sorrow.

From the silent instant of midnight, through all the quiet hours before dawn, and then the cheerfully noisy ones of tomorrow, may this be a merry time for the children, a peaceful time for the old, and a warmly memorable Christmas for all.

May we all make the journey to Bethlehem in spirit, carrying with us a thankful heart as our gift to the Christ.

Deseret News Editorial
Salt Lake City, Utah

---◆---

OVER THE RIVER AND THROUGH THE WOODS

Over the river and thro' the woods,
To grandfather's house we go;
The horse knows the way
To carry the sleigh,
Thro' the white and drifted snow.

Over the river and thro' the woods,
Oh, how the wind does blow!
It stings the toes
And bites the nose
As over the ground we go.

Over the river and thro' the woods,
To have a first-rate play;
Oh hear the bells ring, "Ting-a-ling-ling!"
Hurrah for Thanksgiving Day!

Unknown

---◆---

WHEN THE FROST IS ON THE PUNKIN

When the frost is on the punkin and the fodder's in
the shock,
And you hear the kyouck and gobble of the struttin'
turkey-cock,
And the clackin' of the guineys, and the cluckin' of
the hens,
And the rooster's hallylooyer as he tiptoes on the fence;
Oh, it's then's the times a feller is a-feelin' at his best,
With the risin' sun to greet him from a night of peaceful rest,
As he leaves the house, bareheaded, and goes out to feed
the stock;
When the frost is on the punkin and the fodder's in
the shock.

James Whitcomb Riley

---◆---

Patriotism and Holidays

"You have told us that our day is finished, that we can grow no more and that the future cannot be the equal of the past. But we, the people, do not believe this, and we say to you: Give up the vested interest you have in depression, open your eyes to the future, help us build a new world. We need a new outlook, a new way of getting at things." Thus stated Wendell Willkie. Willkie gathered together in one brief, eloquent statement all the traditional convictions that had been distorted by propaganda and circumstances. He repaired them, reconstituted them and soon they rained down on the citizenry in a torrent, providing solace to the America which, Gunnar Myrdal explains, "is continually struggling for its soul." New frontiers were cited, new resources were developed, plans expanded, and the free enterprise system was back in business at the old stand. The economy spurted ahead, and the poor and discouraged began again to move up the economic ladder under their own steam. Hope was reborn. The clouds blew away, and there again was the future bulging with promise.

I am thinking of you today because it is Christmas, and I
    wish you happiness.
And tomorrow, because it will be the day after Christmas,
    I shall still wish you happiness.
I may not be able to tell you about it every day, because I
    may be far away or we may be very busy.
But that makes no difference — my thoughts and my wishes
    will be with you just the same.
Whatever joy or success comes to you will make me glad
    clear through the year.
I wish you the spirit of Christmas.

Henry Van Dyke

---◆---

On a plaque at the base of the statue of Liberty, which statue was given to the United States by the citizens of France in 1884 and is a universal symbol of the love for freedom shared by these two nations, appear these stirring words by Emma Lazarus:

> "'Keep, ancient lands, your storied pomp!'
> cries she
> With silent lips. 'Give me your tired, your
> poor,
> Your huddled masses yearning to breathe
> free,
> The wretched refuse of your teeming shore.
> Send these, the homeless, tempest-tossed to
> me;
> I lift my lamp beside the golden door.'"

---◆---

At the International Executive Board Meeting of Boy Scouts of America held in Dallas, Texas, on 8 February 1984, John Sloan, from Los Angeles, California, made the following comment: "In Los Angeles we were hosting a 75th anniversary event for Scouting. Curtis LeMay, Secretary of the Air Force, was the invited speaker but could not come. In his place he sent the new commandant of the Air Force Academy. He who introduced the commandant said in his introduction that he had toured the Air Force Academy and that they literally had everything: new buildings, new campus, adequate budget, prestige — everything. A comparison was made with the aging campuses of Annapolis and West Point. As the Commandant commenced speaking he said, 'We have all of the things you mentioned, but one thing we desperately lack: tradition.'"

---◆---

Patriotism and Holidays

The only freedom which deserves the name is that of pursuing our own good in our own way, so long as we do not attempt to deprive others of theirs or impede their efforts to obtain it.

John Stuart Mill

The American Constitution is, as far as I can see, the most wonderful work ever struck off at a given time by the brain and purpose of man.

Wllllam E. Gludslone

Some people talk of "spending" Christmas, others of "observing" Christmas. As Peter Marshall, chaplain of the United States Senate, once put it: "Let's *keep* Christmas. May we keep it in our hearts, that we may be kept in hope."

If there is any principle of the Constitution that more imperatively calls for attachment than any other, it is the principle of free thought — not free thought for those who agree with us, but freedom for the thought that we hate.

Oliver Wendell Holmes

I believe there are more instances of the abridgment of the freedom of the people by gradual and silent encroachment of those in power than by violent and sudden usurpations.

James Madison

The following parody on the 23rd Psalm comes from Cambridge, England, and was written by a Cambridge University Medical Society student: "The government is my shepherd; therefore, I need not work. It alloweth me to lie down on a good job. It leadeth me beside still factories. It destroyeth my initiative. It leadeth me in the path of a parasite for politics' sake. Yea, though I walk through the valley of laziness and deficit spending, I will fear no evil, for the government is with me. It prepareth an economic utopia for me by appropriating the earnings of my own grandchildren. It filleth my head with false security. My inefficiency runneth over. Surely the government should care for me all the days of my life, and I dwell in a fool's paradise forever."

BATTLE HYMN OF THE REPUBLIC

In the beauty of the lilies
Christ was born across the sea,
With a glory in his bosom
That transfigures you and me.
As he died to make men holy
Let us die to make men free,
For God is marching on.

Julia Ward Howe

A distinguished jurist once said: "Freedom cannot be preserved in constitutions if it has vanished from the hearts of its citizens."

Vital Speeches of the Day

Patriotism and Holidays

———————◆———————

I have sworn upon the altar of God, eternal hostility against every form of tyranny over the mind of man.

Thomas Jefferson

———————◆———————

Any society that takes away from those most capable and gives to those least capable will perish.

Abraham Lincoln

———————◆———————

At Christmas time good friends recall
The joys of long ago;
The happy, kindly ways of all
The friends they used to know;
And though some travel far apart
And journey different ways,
All keep a corner in their heart
For happy yesterdays.

Edgar A. Guest

———————◆———————

To preserve our independence we must not let our rulers load us with perpetual debt. We must make our choice between economy and liberty or profusion and servitude. If we run into such debts . . . we must be taxed in our meat and drink, in our necessities and our comforts, in our labors and our amusements. If we can prevent the government from wasting the labors of the people, under the pretense of caring for them, the people will be happy.

Thomas Jefferson

———————◆———————

Patriotism and Holidays

I see America, not in the setting sun of a black night of
despair ahead of us. I see America in the crimson light of
a rising sun, fresh from the burning, creative hand of God.
I see great days ahead, great days possible to men and
women of will and vision.

Carl Sandburg

To open the doors of truth and to fortify the habit of testing
everything by reason are the most effectual manacles we
can rivet on the hands of our successors to prevent their
manacling the people with their own consent.

Thomas Jefferson

Love
and
Service

———————◆———————

Love
and
Service

One of two brothers fighting in the same company in France fell by an enemy bullet. The one who escaped asked permission of his officer to go and bring his brother in.

"He is probably dead," said the officer, "and there is no use in you risking your life to bring in his body."

However, after further pleading, the officer consented. Just as the soldier reached the lines with his brother on his shoulders, the wounded man died.

"There, you see," said the officer, "you risked your life for nothing."

"No," replied the soldier. "I did what he expected of me, and I have my reward. When I crept up to him and took him in my arms, he said, 'Tom, I knew you would come; I just felt you would come.'"

The Scouter's Minute

Remember this: No man is a failure who has friends.

199

JET DETOURS TO RESCUE INJURED BOY

An Alaska Airlines nonstop flight carrying 150 passengers was diverted to a remote town on a mercy mission to rescue a badly injured boy.

Two-year-old Elton Williams, III, had severed an artery in his arm when he fell on a piece of glass while playing near his home Wednesday in Yakutat, 450 miles south of Anchorage.

Medics at the scene asked the airline to evacuate the boy. As a result, the Anchorage-to-Seattle flight was diverted to Yakutat.

The medics said the boy was bleeding badly and probably would not live through the flight to Seattle, so the plane flew 200 miles to Juneau, the nearest city with a hospital. The flight then went on to Seattle with the passengers arriving two hours late, most missing their connections. But none complained. In fact, they dug into their pocket-books and took up a $150 collection for the boy and his family.

Later, as the flight was about to land in Seattle, the passengers broke into a cheer when the pilot said he had received word by radio that Elton was going to be all right.

Deseret News
Salt Lake City, Utah

Although we treasure newer friends,
We cannot forget the old.
The new ones are like silver,
The old ones purest gold.

Love and Service

Where human institutions are concerned, love without criticism brings stagnation, and criticism without love brings destruction. The swifter the pace of change, the more lovingly men must care for and criticize their institutions to keep them intact through the turbulent passages.

John Gardner

FOR WHOM THE BELL TOLLS

No man is an island, entire of itself; every man is a piece of the continent, a part of the main. If a clod be washed away by the sea, Europe is the less, as well as if a promontory were, as well as if a manor of thy friend's or of thine own were: any man's death diminishes me, because I am involved in mankind, and therefore never send to know for whom the bell tolls; it tolls for thee.

John Donne

PEOPLE LIKED HIM

People liked him, not because
He was rich or known to fame;
He had never won applause
As a star in any game.
His was not a brilliant style;
His was not a forceful way.
But he had a gentle smile
And a kindly word to say.

Edgar A. Guest

I KNOW SOMETHING GOOD ABOUT YOU

Wouldn't this old world be better
If the folks we meet would say —
"I know something good about you!"
And treat us just that way?

Wouldn't it be fine and dandy
If each handclasp, fond and true,
Carried with it this assurance —
"I know something good about you!"

Wouldn't life be lots more happy
If the good that's in us all
Were the only thing about us
That folks bothered to recall?

Wouldn't life be lots more happy
If we praised the good we see?
For there's such a lot of goodness
In the worst of you and me!

Wouldn't it be nice to practice
That fine way of thinking, too?
You know something good about me,
I know something good about you.

Unknown

Today I stood among the tall trees and now I am taller.

He who pushes you closer to God — he is your friend.

Often we live side by side but not heart to heart.

An elderly man disclosed at the funeral of his brother, with whom he had shared, from early manhood, a small one-room cabin near Canisteo, New York, that following a quarrel, they had divided the room in half with a chalk line and neither had crossed the line nor spoken a word to the other since that day — sixty-two years before!

He that cannot forgive others breaks the bridge over which he himself must pass if he would ever reach heaven; for everyone has need to be forgiven.

George Herbert

NOT UNDERSTOOD

Not understood. Poor souls with stunted vision
Oft measure giants by their narrow gauge;
The poisoned shafts of falsehood and derision
Are oft impelled 'gainst those who mould the age —
Not understood.

Not understood. How many breasts are aching
For lack of sympathy! Ah, day to day
How many cheerless, lonely hearts are breaking!
How many noble spirits pass away —
Not understood.

O God! that men would see a little clearer,
Or judge less harshly where they cannot see;
O God! that men would draw a little nearer
To one another; they'd be nearer Thee —
And understood.

Thomas Bracken

The second most destructive weapon is the gun. The first? The human tongue.

William George Jordan

PASS IT ON

Have you had a kindness shown?
Pass it on.

'Twas not given for thee alone.
Pass it on.

Let it travel down the years,
Let it wipe another's tears,
Till in heaven the deed appears.
Pass it on.

Henry K. Burton

The greatness of a man can nearly always be measured by his willingness to be kind.

George W. Young

HIAWATHA'S WOOING

As unto the bow the cord is,
So unto the man is woman,
Though she bends him, she obeys him,
Though she draws him, yet she follows,
Useless each without the other!

Henry Wadsworth Longfellow

Love and Service

---◆---

True Christianity is love in action.

David O. McKay

---◆---

MAKE THE WORLD BRIGHTER

Go gladden the lonely, the dreary;
Go comfort the weeping, the weary;
Go scatter kind deeds on your way.
Oh, make the world brighter today!

Mrs. Frank A. Breck

---◆---

Love gives itself; it is not bought.

Henry Wadsworth Longfellow

---◆---

Where "thank you" is seldom heard it is doubly
appreciated.

---◆---

Getting along well with other people is still the world's
most needed skill. With it . . . there is no limit to what a
person can do. We need people; we need the cooperation
of others. There is very little that we can do alone.

Earl Nightingale

---◆---

The late Dr. Abraham Maslow said that one judges a person
the same way he judges an apple tree: Look at what he
produces or has produced and judge him by that.

---◆---

◆

Most people have a need to be needed.

Royal Bank of Canada Newsletter

◆

The gift of love is about the only present that isn't exchanged after Christmas.

Kenneth Parsons

◆

When you help someone up a hill, you are a little nearer the top yourself.

◆

I looked at my brother with the microscope of criticism, and I said, "How coarse my brother is."

I looked at my brother with the telescope of scorn, and I said, "How small my brother is."

Then I looked into the mirror of truth, and I said, "How like me my brother is."

◆

Inscription on the wall of the Library of Congress: "Mercy is the characteristic virtue of a great man."

◆

We must go on until we are perfect, loving our neighbor more than we love ourselves. It is folly in the extreme for persons to say that they love God when they do not love their brethren.

Brigham Young

◆

Love and Service

We look forward to the time when the power of love will replace the love of power. Then will our world know the blessings of peace.

William E. Gladstone

It is better to save the life of a man than to raise one from the dead.

Joseph Smith

Inscription on a monument at Guadalcanal where, during World War II, a U.S. Marine regiment was totally annihilated: "When you go home, tell them, and say, 'For their tomorrows, we gave our today.'"

GOD'S LOVE

We do not see the wind,
We only hear it sigh;
It makes the grasses bend
Whenever it goes by.

We do not see God's love,
But in our hearts we know
He watches over us
Wherever we may go.

We do not have to see
To know the wind is here;
We do not have to see
To know God's love is near.

Elizabeth Cushing Taylor

"For I am persuaded, that neither death, nor life, nor angels, nor principalities, nor powers, nor things present, nor things to come, nor height, nor depth, nor any other creature, shall be able to separate us from the love of God, which is in Christ Jesus our Lord."

Romans 8:38-39

They do not love who do not show their love.

William Shakespeare

OUTWITTED

He drew a circle that shut me out—
Heretic, rebel, a thing to flout.
But Love and I had the wit to win:
We drew a circle that took him in.

Edwin Markham

A CREED

There is a destiny that makes us brothers;
None goes his way alone:
All that we send into the lives of others
Comes back into our own.

Edwin Markham

"When ye are in the service of your fellow beings ye are only in the service of your God."

Mosiah 2:17

Love and Service

◆

Ah! when shall all men's good
Be each man's rule, and universal peace
Lie like a shaft of light across the land.

Alfred, Lord Tennyson

◆

No one can reach everybody, but everybody can be reached by somebody.

◆

Tolerance without compromising truth or principles is one of the great needs of our time.

Richard L. Evans

◆

Men should take care not to make women weep, for God counts their tears.

◆

Be to her faults a little blind, and to her virtues over kind.

Alexander Pope

◆

Boys flying kites call them their white-winged birds;
You can't do that when you're flying words.
Thoughts unexpressed may sometimes fall back dead,
But God Himself can't kill them once they're said.

◆

Nothing is so strong as gentleness, and nothing is so gentle as real strength.

◆

HEAVY-HEARTED OBSERVER

Yesterday was an old man's birthday. He was 91. He awakened earlier than usual, bathed, shaved and put on his best clothes. Surely they would come today, he thought.

He didn't take his daily walk to the gas station to visit with the old-timers of the community, because he wanted to be right there when they came.

He sat on the front porch with a clear view of the road so he could see them coming. Surely they would come today. He decided to skip his noon nap because he wanted to be up when they came.

He has six children.

Two of his daughters and their married children live within four miles. They hadn't been to see him for such a long time. But today was his birthday. Surely they would come today.

At suppertime he refused to cut the cake and asked that the ice cream be left in the freezer. He wanted to wait and have dessert with *them* when they came.

About nine o'clock he went to his room and got ready for bed. His last words before turning out the lights were, "Promise to wake me up when they come."

It was his birthday, and he was 91.

Unknown

It does not pay to scold. I believe you can get people to do anything (if you can get them to do it at all) by loving them into doing it.

George Albert Smith

Love and Service

The Gospel would give peace to the world just as surely as it does to a family or to an individual, if the world would receive it. There is one, and only one, way by which a universal and lasting peace can be secured to the nations of the earth and that is by their submitting to the dictation and government of the King of peace and by bowing in obedience to the principles which He has enunciated.

George Q. Cannon

A man filled with the love of God is not content with blessing his family alone but ranges through the whole world anxious to bless the whole human race.

Joseph Smith

SONNETS FROM THE PORTUGUESE
(XLIII)

How do I love thee? Let me count the ways.
I love thee to the depth and breadth and height
My soul can reach, when feeling out of sight
For the ends of Being and ideal Grace.
I love thee to the level of everyday's
Most quiet need, by sun and candle-light.
I love thee freely, as men strive for Right;
I love thee purely, as they turn from Praise.
I love thee with the passion put to use
In my old griefs, and with my childhood's faith.
I love thee with a love I seemed to lose
With my lost saints—I love thee with the breath,
Smiles, tears, of all my life!—and, if God choose,
I shall but love thee better after death.

Elizabeth Barrett Browning

Love and Service

◆

The United States Post Office dead letter department receives annually thousands and thousands of children's pre-Christmas letters addressed to Santa Claus asking for things. After it was all over one year, a single, solitary letter thanking Santa Claus was received.

Could this be one of the problems of this troubled world—that people think only of getting, not giving; of receiving, and not even expressing their gratitude for that which they do receive?

Margaret R. Jackson

◆

True happiness comes only by making others happy—the practical application of the Savior's doctrine of losing one's life to gain it.

David O. McKay

◆

TO KNOW ALL IS TO FORGIVE ALL

If I knew you and you knew me—
If both of us could clearly see,
And with an inner sight divine
The meaning of your heart and mine—
I'm sure that we would differ less
And clasp our hands in friendliness;
Our thoughts would pleasantly agree
If I knew you, and you knew me.

Nixon Waterman

◆

Love and Service

◆

They also serve who only stand and wait.

John Milton

◆

"There is no peace, saith the Lord, unto the wicked."

Isaiah 48:22

◆

ABOU BEN ADHEM

Abou Ben Adhem (may his tribe increase!)
Awoke one night from a deep dream of peace,
And saw, within the moonlight in his room,
Making it rich, and like a lily in bloom,
An Angel writing in a book of gold:
Exceeding peace had made Ben Adhem bold,
And to the Presence in the room he said:
"What writest thou?" The Vision raised its head,
And with a look made of all sweet accord
Answered, "The names of those who love the Lord."
"And is mine one?" said Abou. "Nay, not so,"
Replied the Angel. Abou spoke more low,
But cheerily still; and said, "I pray thee, then,
Write me as one that loves his fellow men."

The Angel wrote, and vanished. The next night
It came again with a great wakening light,
And showed the names whom love of God had blessed,
And, lo! Ben Adhem's name led all the rest!

James Henry Leigh Hunt

◆

LITTLE THINGS

Little drops of water,
Little grains of sand,
Make the mighty ocean
And the pleasant land.

So the little moments,
Humble though they be,
Make the mighty ages
Of eternity.

So our little errors
Lead the soul away
From the path of virtue
Far in sin to stray.

Little deeds of kindness,
Little words of love,
Help to make earth happy
Like the heaven above.

Julia Fletcher Carney

It isn't easy for those who are young to understand the loneliness that comes when life changes from a time of preparation and performance to a time of putting things away. In the eager and active years of youth, it isn't easy to understand how parents feel as their flock, one by one, leave the family fireside. To be so long the center of a home, so much sought after, and then, almost suddenly, to be on the sidelines watching the procession pass by—this is living into loneliness.

Of course we may think we are thoughtful of parents and of our other older folk. Don't we send them gifts and

---

messages on special days and anniversaries? And don't we make an occasional quick call as a token of our attention? It is something to be remembered on special occasions, to be sure. But passing and perfunctory performances are not enough to keep loneliness in its place the whole year round.

What they need in the loneliness of their older years is, in part at least, what we needed in the uncertain years of our youth: a sense of belonging, an assurance of being wanted, and the kindly ministrations of loving hearts and hands; not merely dutiful formality, not merely a room in a building, but room in someone's heart and life. We have to live a long time to learn how empty a room can be that is filled only with furniture. It takes someone on whom we have claims beyond mere hired service, beyond institutional care or professional duty, to thaw out the memories of the past and keep them warmly living in the present.

And we who are young should never become so blindly absorbed in our own pursuits as to forget that there are still with us those who will live in loneliness unless we let them share our lives as once they let us share theirs. When they were moving in the mainstream of their own impelling affairs, we were a burden — or could have been if they had chosen to consider us as such. But now we are stronger, and they are less strong. We cannot bring them back the morning hours of youth. But we can help them live in the warm glow of a sunset made more beautiful by our thoughtfulness, by our provision, and by our active and unfeigned love.

Life in its fullness is a loving ministry of service from generation to generation. God grant that those who belong to us may never be left in loneliness.

Richard L. Evans

THE TOUCH OF THE MASTER'S HAND

'Twas battered and scarred, and the auctioneer
Thought it scarcely worth his while
To waste much time on the old violin,
But held it up with a smile:
"What am I bidden, good folks," he cried,
"Who'll start the bidding for me?"
"A dollar, a dollar"; then, "Two!" "Only two?
Two dollars, and who'll make it three?
Three dollars, once; three dollars, twice;
going for three——" But no,
From the room, far back, a gray-haired man
Came forward and picked up the bow;
Then, wiping the dust from the old violin,
And tightening the loose strings,
He played a melody pure and sweet
As a caroling angel sings.

The music ceased, and the auctioneer,
With a voice that was quiet and low,
Said: "What am I bid for the old violin?"
And he held it up with the bow.
"A thousand dollars, and who'll make it two?
Two thousand! And who'll make it three?
Three thousand, once, three thousand, twice,
And going, and gone," said he.
The people cheered, but some of them cried,
"We do not quite understand
What changed its worth." Swift came the reply:
"The touch of a master's hand."

And many a man with life out of tune,
And battered and scarred with sin,
Is auctioned cheap to the thoughtless crowd,

Much like the old violin.
A "mess of pottage," a glass of wine;
A game — and he travels on.
He is "going" once, "going" twice,
He's "going" and almost "gone."
But the Master comes, and the foolish crowd
Never can quite understand
The worth of a soul and the change that's wrought
By the touch of the Master's hand.

Myra Brooks Welch

THE MAKING OF FRIENDS

If nobody smiled and nobody cheered and nobody
    helped us along,
If each every minute looked after himself and good things
    all went to the strong,
If nobody cared just a little for you, and nobody thought
    about me,
And we all stood alone in the battle of life,
What a dreary old world this would be!

Life is sweet because of the friends we have made and the
    things which in common we share;
We want to live on not because of ourselves, but because
    of the people who care;
It's giving and doing for somebody else — on that all life's
    splendor depends,
And the joy of this world, when you've summed it all up,
Is found in the making of friends.

Edgar A. Guest

———————————◆———————————

Blessed are they who have the gift of making friends: the power of going out of one's self and appreciating whatever is noble and loving in another.

Thomas Hughes

———————————◆———————————

NEW FRIENDS AND OLD FRIENDS

Make new friends, but keep the old;
Those are silver, these are gold.
New-made friendships, like new wine,
Age will mellow and refine.
Friendships that have stood the test—
Time and change—are surely best.
Brow may wrinkle, hair grow gray;
Friendship never knows decay;
For, 'mid old friends, tried and true,
Once more we our youth renew.
But old friends, alas! may die;
New friends must their place supply.
Cherish friendship in your breast;
New is good, but old is best.
Make new friends, but keep the old;
Those are silver, these are gold.

Joseph Parry

———————————◆———————————

A true friend is the greatest of all blessings and the one which we take the least thought to acquire.

———————————◆———————————

Life
and
Learning

Life
and
Learning

There is great ability in knowing how to conceal one's ability.

Maslow advances what he calls the "Jonah" complex: the tendency in adults to doubt and even fear their own abilities, their own potential to be greater. We fear our highest possibilities (as well as our lowest ones). We are generally afraid to become that which we can glimpse in our most perfect conditions, under conditions of greatest courage. We enjoy and even thrill to the godlike possibilities we see in ourselves in such peak moments. And yet we simultaneously shiver with weakness, awe and fear for these very same possibilities.

Earl Nightingale

Adversity is sometimes hard upon a man; but for one man who can stand prosperity, there are a hundred that will stand adversity.

Thomas Carlyle

At the relief of Dunkirk, a motor torpedo boat sped away from England to pick up its quota of beleaguered British and French soldiers. The signalman on shore flashed to it: "Good luck."

The captain replied: "Thanks. Actually, we rely on skill."

Prosperity doth best discover vice, but adversity doth best discover virtue.

Francis Bacon

A man never shows his own character so plainly as by his manner of portraying another's.

Johann Paul Richter

See how the masses of man worry themselves into nameless graves, while here and there a great, unselfish soul forgets himself into immortality.

Ralph Waldo Emerson

Man is a builder, first of his own character, then of his family, his community and his nation. The specifications from which he must build are not really a mystery, for God's word, if one seeks it, is loud and clear: "Except the Lord build the house," said the Psalmist, "they labor in vain that build it."

Nation's Business

Life and Learning

◆

The world of books is the most remarkable creation of man; nothing else that he builds ever lasts. Monuments fall; nations perish; civilizations grow old and die out. After an era of darkness, new races build others; but in the world of books are volumes that live on as young and fresh as the day they were written, still telling men's hearts of the hearts of men centuries dead.

Clarence Day

◆

A man is himself, plus what he reads.

Parkes Cadman

◆

Inscription on the wall of the Library of Congress: "In books lies the soul of the whole passed time."

◆

Character is what one is; reputation is what one has done.

◆

Personality is persistent; death cannot touch the spirit of man.

David O. McKay

◆

A man with knowledge and great moral principles is a great man; but a man with knowledge and no moral principles is only a clever devil.

Dwight D. Eisenhower

◆

When wealth is lost, nothing is lost; when health is lost, something is lost; when character is lost, all is lost.

A person of character is one who likes and dislikes what he ought. He is honest by habit and as a matter of course. He has been taught this way of living by parents who did not ask him, "What will people think?" but, rather, "What will you think of yourself?"

A game of golf cannot be enjoyed on a course that is all fairway, without any rough, any trees, any water hazard or sand traps. It is the obstacles that make it a game.

Royal Bank of Canada Newsletter

Advice is like snow: the softer it falls, the longer it dwells upon and the deeper it sinks into the mind.

Samuel Taylor Coleridge

Inscription on the wall of the Library of Congress: "We taste the spices of Arabia yet never feel the scorching sun which brings them forth."

Books: Some are to be tasted, others to be swallowed and some few to be chewed and digested.

Francis Bacon

THE FEW

The easy roads are crowded,
And the level roads are jammed;
The pleasant little rivers
With the drifting folks are crammed.
But off yonder where it's rocky,
Where you get a better view,
You will find the ranks are thinning
And the travelers are few.

Where the going's smooth and pleasant
You will always find the throng,
For the many, more's the pity,
Seem to like to drift along.
But the steeps that call for courage,
And the task that's hard to do,
In the end result in glory
For the never-wavering few.

Edgar A. Guest

A lighthouse with no light is worse than no lighthouse at all.

"The Lord seeth not as man seeth; for man looketh on the outward appearance, but the Lord looketh on the heart."

1 Samuel 16:7

Our complacency tree has many branches, and each spring more buds come into bloom.

BOOKS ARE KEYS

Books are keys to wisdom's treasure;
Books are gates to lands of pleasure;
Books are paths that upward lead;
Books are friends. Come, let us read.

Emilie Poulsson

Conscience warns us as a friend before it punishes us as a judge.

Stanislaus

A nation without a conscience is a nation without a soul. A nation without a soul is a nation that cannot live.

Sir Winston Churchill

President Joseph F. Smith warned the Latter-day Saints of three dangers to avoid: (1) flattery of worldly men; (2) false educational theories; (3) sexual immorality.

God's finger touch'd him, and he slept.

Alfred, Lord Tennyson

We shall miss him much; there was so much to miss.

Richard L. Evans

226

———————————————◆———————————————

Said one young man from an affluent family: Most people don't think any changes are needed in an affluent community. We have *everything*, they say. But I guess you have to be rich to really understand that money doesn't buy everything. Values, for example.

Money can't buy you character, self-reliance, physical fitness, mental awareness. Money can't teach you how to live with people. Things like that can't be bought. Only taught.

In the affluent community, we're conscious of our responsibility to business, industry, and politics. Learning how to direct our resources wisely is a high priority. We don't have to keep up with change. We have to keep ahead of it.

———————————————◆———————————————

He is poor who has nothing but money.

———————————————◆———————————————

The fate of the country . . . does not depend on what kind of paper you drop into the ballot box once a year, but on what kind of man you drop from your chamber into the street every morning.

Henry David Thoreau

———————————————◆———————————————

Quotations inscribed on the John L. Vestal School Building, Portland, Oregon: "The child is heir to the wisdom of all the ages. This is his treasure house."

"The child has infinite possibilities. Here he may realize some of them."

———————————————◆———————————————

CROSSING THE BAR

Sunset and evening star,
And one clear call for me,
And may there be no moaning of the bar,
When I put out to sea.

But such a tide as moving seems asleep,
Too full for sound and foam,
When that which drew from out the boundless deep
Turns again home.

Twilight and evening bell,
And after that the dark!
And may there be no sadness of farewell,
When I embark;

For tho' from out our bourne of time and place
The flood may bear me far,
I hope to see my Pilot face to face
When I have crossed the bar.

Alfred, Lord Tennyson

Education does not mean teaching people to know what
they do not know; it means teaching them to behave as
they do not behave.

John Ruskin

AN ESSAY ON CRITICISM

A little learning is a dangerous thing;
Drink deep or taste not the Pierian spring.

Alexander Pope

Life and Learning

———————◆———————

A friend of mine a while ago came across an interesting relic of the Old West: the last will and testament of a rugged frontiersman. It was crudely made but left a great legacy to his son. "This here," he wrote, "is my last will and testament. I ain't got no money to leave you, nothing exceptin' our old cabin, Old Buck [which was probably his horse], and my two guns. But I do leave you somethin' worth a parcel more than money: (1) A man's word that is as good as his bond; (2) faith in God; (3) courage, so you won't be afraid of nothin' or nobody."

Honesty, faith and courage! What a priceless legacy that is! Euripedes said that courage can be taught, as a child is taught to speak. And I rather think that is just what the frontiersman was trying to say. His example would serve his son better than a pouch full of gold; and he was right.

Norman Vincent Peale

———————◆———————

What lies behind you and what lies before you are insignificant compared to what lies within you.

———————◆———————

The ultimate aim of education is the training of character.

Plato

———————◆———————

The boss handed the new employee a broom. "Sweep up that mess in the stockroom," he commanded.

"But sir," objected the employee, "I'm a college graduate."

"Oh well; in that case," replied the employer, "come—I'll show you how!"

———————◆———————

There is never a life without sadness,
There is never a heart free from pain;
If one seeks in this world for true solace,
He seeks it forever in vain.

So when to your heart comes the sorrow
Of losing some dear one you've known,
'Tis the touch of God's sickle at harvest
Since He reaps in the fields He has sown.

Whom, then, do I call educated? First, those who control circumstances instead of being mastered by them; those who meet all occasions manfully and act in accordance with intelligent thinking; those who are honorable in all dealings, who treat good-naturedly persons and things that are disagreeable; and furthermore, those who hold their pleasures under control and are not overcome by misfortune; finally, those who are not spoiled by success.

Socrates

A great mind is one that is neither ancient nor modern; it is neither ashamed of the old nor afraid of the new. It thinks neither in terms of old traditions nor in terms of new fashions. It is only concerned with the true and the workable.

N. Eldon Tanner

All men by nature desire knowledge.

Aristotle

Life and Learning

TWO TEMPLES

A Builder builded a temple,
He wrought it with grace and skill;
Pillars and groins and arches
All fashioned to work his will.
Men said, as they saw its beauty,
"It shall never know decay;
Great is thy skill, O Builder!
Thy fame shall endure for aye."

A teacher builded a temple
With loving and infinite care,
Planning each arch with patience,
Laying each stone with prayer.
None praised her unceasing efforts,
None knew of her wondrous plan,
For the temple the teacher builded
Was unseen by the eyes of man.

Gone is the builder's temple,
Crumbled into dust.
Low lies each stately pillar,
Food for consuming rust.
But the temple the teacher builded
Will last while the ages roll,
For that beautiful, unseen temple
Was a child's immortal soul.

Hattie Bose Hall

A building which houses archives has printed on its facade
the phrase from Shakespeare's *Tempest:* "What's past is
prologue." In the play, Antonio completes his comment by
saying, "What is to come is in our hands."

Royal Bank of Canada Newsletter

231

great homage to fallen leaders. But why is it that man cannot always devise the means to show a living person how deeply he is loved, respected, and admired. Death has taken a mountain of a man from our midst. As general, former President Dwight David Eisenhower comes home to Abilene for the final time. Let us resolve to live in keeping with the spirit of a man whose respect for others made him humble enough to listen and to understand, yet kept him firm in his own beliefs.

Walt Lockman

IN MEMORY OF JOHN P. MALMBERG
(1827 — 1881)

A light from our household is gone;
A voice we loved is stilled;
A place is vacant in our hearts
That never can be filled.

Tilford Moots went to the Poorhouse the other day to visit a friend who tried to publish a newspaper that pleased everybody.

Harvey Jacobs

Fear . . . it knows no master but one. His name is Understanding.

---◆---

REQUIEM

Under the wide and starry sky
Dig the grave and let me lie.
Glad did I live and gladly die,
And I laid me down with a will.

This be the verse you grave for me:
Here he lies where he longed to be;
Home is the sailor, home from the sea,
And the hunter home from the hill.

Robert Louis Stevenson

---◆---

The man walking down the street carrying a cat by the tail is gaining at least ten times as much experience as the man who is just standing there watching him.

Mark Twain

---◆---

I don't think much of a man no wiser today than he was yesterday.

Abraham Lincoln

---◆---

The three C's of failure: Criticism, Condemnation, and Complaining.

The three C's of success: Compassion, Courage, and Commitment.

---◆---

Never entertain any thought of failure.

---◆---

Fear is usually the product of incomplete knowledge or incomplete thinking.

Of all the liars in the world, sometimes the worst are your own fears.

Rudyard Kipling

"With some I am not well pleased, for they will not open their mouths, but they hide the talent which I have given unto them, because of the fear of man."

D&C 60:2

In 1587 Sir Francis Drake stopped a Spanish merchant fleet. Its cargo was strange: seasoned oak barrel staves. Drake reasoned they would be used to carry provisions in an attack on England. He burned them. A year later the Armada sailed. Its food, in green, unseasoned barrels, spoiled. Spain's crews sickened. Drake's foresight, more than the battle itself, sent a mighty empire into decline. Luck may bring us opportunity; intelligence alone shapes it to our purposes.

Royal Bank of Canada Newsletter

A sophisticated economy, based upon power tools and computers, upon the engineer and the professional, has no room at the bottom for unskilled labor. "The uneducated need not apply," is the unseen sign on every employment door.

Life and Learning

Education is not just a luxury permitting some men an advantage over others. It has become a necessity without which a person is defenseless in this complex, industrialized society. We have truly entered the century of the educated man.

Lyndon B. Johnson

An educated man is not one whose memory is trained to carry a few dates in history. He is one who can accomplish things. A man who cannot think is not an educated man, however many college degrees he may have acquired. Thinking is the hardest work anyone can do, which is probably the reason why we have so few thinkers.

Henry Ford

Credit hours, transcripts, satisfied requirements and diplomas do not an education make. Education is a process, not a completed act. The prescriptions of our time look as though you will be exposed to acquiring an education whether you like it or not. You don't need to ask any more for an educational opportunity. You have only to knock to take advantage of it. But to achieve excellence, you must open the door to learning yourself. Contrary to what we would like to believe, excellence in education is rarely unearned.

Education is derived from the Latin word, *educarri*, which means "to draw out."

◆

The society which scorns excellence in plumbing because plumbing is a humble activity and tolerates shoddiness in philosophy because it is an exalted activity will have neither good plumbing nor good philosophy. Neither its pipes nor its theories will hold water.

John Gardner

◆

A young agricultural graduate looked over a farmer's field and criticized his method of cultivation. "Why, I'd be surprised if you get ten tons of beets from this field," he said.

"So would I," the farmer replied. "That's a potato field!"

◆

The past is behind; learn from it. The future is before us; prepare for it.

Weber

◆

The one thing we learn from experience is that we don't learn from experience.

George Bernard Shaw

◆

Neither wealth, nor fame, nor any other instrument of power can ever be more reliable in assuring our security and peace of mind than the knowledge of having inspired gratitude in a great many people.

Dr. Hans Selye

◆

Life and Learning

---◆---

AWAY

I cannot say, and I will not say
That he is dead. He is just away!
With a cheery smile, and a wave of the hand,
He has wandered into an unknown land,
And left us dreaming how very fair
It needs must be, since he lingers there.
And you—O you, who the wildest yearn
For the old-time step and the glad return,
Think of him faring on, as dear
In the love of There as the love of Here;
And loyal still, as he gave the blows
Of his warrior-strength to his country's foes.
Mild and gentle, as he was brave,
When the sweetest love of his life he gave
To simple things: Where the violets grew
Blue as the eyes they were liken to,
The touches of his hands have strayed
As reverently as his lips have prayed:
When the little brown thrush that harshly chirred
Was dear to him as the mocking-bird;
And he pitied as much as a man in pain
A writhing honey-bee wet with rain.
Think of him still as the same, I say:
He is not dead—he is just away!

James Whitcomb Riley

---◆---

Education must begin with the teacher. Someone once said that the teacher is the "backbone" of our nation. I would prefer to say that the teacher is the living heart of the nation.

Dr. Lena B. Prewitt

---◆---

———————◆———————

No man need fear death; he need fear only that he may die without having known his greatest power — the power of his free will to give of his life to others. If something comes to life in others because of you, then you have made an approach to immortality.

Norman Cousins

———————◆———————

Just before an offensive by United States troops into Germany during World War II, General Dwight D. Eisenhower was asked to offer impromptu words of encouragement. Rain had fallen earlier, and several GI carpenters had hammered together a rude platform on a mound.

After some cheering remarks, Ike stepped off the platform onto a mound of slick gumbo. His feet slipped out from under him, and he took a spectacular pratfall. The troops hollered and laughed.

Most commanders would have reprimanded the troops for such behavior. General Eisenhower, however, merely got back on his feet, brushed himself off, turned to the troops, saluted them and smiled his famous smile. The result? Those troops let loose with a chorus of cheers that could be heard in Berlin.

Virgil Pinkley

———————◆———————

This is the law of benefits between men: The one ought to forget at once what he has given, and the other ought never to forget what he has received.

Lucius Annaeus Seneca

———————◆———————

LETTER TO MRS. LYDIA BIXBY

Dear Madam,

I have just been shown in the Files of the War Department a statement of the Adjutant General of Massachusetts that you are the mother of five sons who have died gloriously on the field of battle. I feel how weak and fruitless must be any words of mine which should attempt to beguile you from the grief of a loss so overwhelming. But I cannot refrain from tendering to you the consolation that may be found in the thanks of the Republic they died to save. I pray that our heavenly Father may assuage the anguish of your bereavement, and leave you only the cherished memory of the loved and lost, and the solemn pride that must be yours to have laid so costly a sacrifice upon the altar of freedom.

> Yours very sincerely and respectfully,
> A. Lincoln

General George S. Patton's favorite quotation — the one that his wife, Bea, used as dedication for her husband's account of World War II, *War As I Knew It* — gives the very flavor of the man and soldier:

THE PILGRIM'S PROGRESS

"My sword I give to him that shall succeed me in my pilgrimage, and my courage and skill to him that can get it. My works and scars I carry with me, to be a witness for me that I have fought his battles who now will be my rewarder." So he passed over, and all the trumpets sounded for him on the other side . . .

John Bunyan

———————————◆———————————

Inscriptions at the American Memorial Cemetery of the Philippines:

"Take unto thyself, O Lord, the souls of the valiant."

"Some there be which have no sepulchre; their name liveth for evermore."

"Grant unto them, O Lord, eternal rest who sleep in unknown graves."

"Let us here highly resolve that the cause for which they died shall live."

"Comrades in arms, whose earthly resting place is known only to God."

"To their memory, their country brings its gratitude as flowers forever living."

"O Lord, support us all the day long until the shadows lengthen and our work is done. Then in Thy mercy grant us a safe lodging and a holy rest and peace at the last."

———————————◆———————————

Great ideas come into the world as gently as doves. Perhaps then if we listen attentively we shall hear, amid the uproar of empires and nations, a faint flutter of wings, the gentle stirring of life and hope.

Albert Camus

———————————◆———————————

It has been determined that the best age for learning is in the twenties. An individual's ability to learn increases up to the age of twenty-two, remains the same to thirty-five and is still high at fifty.

Dr. Ed D. Smith & Sons Newsletter

———————————◆———————————

Life and Learning

The Crusades, the whole legal and ecclesiastical fiction of feudalism, laboriously contrived and stunningly staged, soon degenerated into a sordid free-for-all in which those who sought to possess this world and the other at once, wearing the armor of conquest beneath the sacrosanct robes of unworldly pilgrims, ended up possessing neither.

Ill habits gather by unseen degrees —
As brooks make rivers, rivers run to seas.

John Dryden

Good habits are the soul's muscles. The more you use them, the stronger they grow.

Bad habits: First we could break them if we would; then we would break them if we could.

Habits are chains that are too small to be felt until they are too strong to be broken.

Samuel Johnson

Whatever part you choose to play on the world stage, keep in mind that life is like a candid camera: It does not wait for you to pose. You cannot adopt safely the Bohemian belief that washing the dishes should be left until they are needed.

Royal Bank of Canada Newsletter

The happy life is not ushered in at any age to the sound of drums and trumpets. It grows upon us year by year, little by little, until at last we realize that we have it. It is achieved in individuals not by flights to the moon or Mars, but by a body of work done so well that we can lift our heads with assurance and look the universe in the eye. Of this be sure: You do not find the happy life — you make it.

Royal Bank of Canada Newsletter

Keep your face turned always toward the sunlight, and the shadows will fall behind you.

Don't let life discourage you. Everyone who got where he is had to begin where he was.

Ask a woman how she stubbed her toe, and she'll say she walked into a chair; ask a man, and he'll say someone left a chair in the middle of the room.

Lufkin Industries ROUNDUP

People are forever buying things they don't need, with money they don't have, to please people they don't like.

Will Rogers

He is rich according to what he is — not according to what he has.

Henry Ward Beecher

---◆---

One of literature's best-loved characters, Anne of Green Gables, stated: "Looking forward to things is half the pleasure of them."

---◆---

Happiness is the desire of most people. But the number of folks who miss it is appalling. Instead of living in the sunshine of happiness, they are dwelling under the cloud of gloom. The road they follow leads to the swamp of despair instead of the garden of happiness. This need not be. There are a few simple rules that, if followed, will produce happiness. They are:

1. Keep your mind stored with constructive thoughts.
2. Look for the beautiful and pleasant things in life.
3. Adjust yourself to whatever happens in life so as to make the best of it.
4. Have no regrets — live in the present instead of the past.
5. Give every man a square deal, whether he be prince or pauper.
6. Do your job, no matter how humble it may be, with the best efforts you can give.
7. Do something for someone every day.
8. Have faith in yourself, your fellows and God.

---◆---

To measure the goodness of life by its delights, pleasures, and safety is to apply a false standard. The happy life doesn't consist of a glut of luxury. It does not make itself content with commercially produced pleasure — the nightclub idea of what is a good time — mistaking it for happiness. The happy life is made up of substantial things and attributes and purposes. To be sure, you do not find the happy life; you make it!

Royal Bank of Canada Newsletter

---◆---

Life and Learning

◆

We should be careful to get out of an experience only the wisdom that is in it — and stop there; lest we be like the cat that sits down on a hot stove lid. She will never sit down on a hot stove lid again — and that is well; but also she will never sit down on a cold one any more.

Mark Twain

◆

One must, having learned to learn, go on learning. What the public takes for brilliance is really the result of thorough, painstaking investigation and downright hard work. We may well rejoice that work is not reserved for slaves. If that were the case, we should be robbed of our greatest field of enjoyment, and we should be forever condemned to mediocrity.

Royal Bank of Canada Newsletter

◆

Learn enthusiasm from youth — young people possess it in
  abundance.
Learn wisdom from the mature — they have experienced
  much.
Learn understanding from God — He knows the end from
  the beginning.
Learn integrity from oneself — let your conscience be your
  guide.

◆

The fastest and best method of finding the answer to a simple problem is often through trial and error. This axiom is disputed by many women, who think talking about it is more interesting, and by many men, who think they should refer it to a committee.

Edward Hodnett

◆

Life and Learning

◆

In the time of your life, live so that in good time there shall be no ugliness or death for yourself or for any life your life touches.

William Saroyan

◆

"Strait is the gate, and narrow is the way, which leadeth unto life, and few there be that find it."

Matthew 7:14

◆

One of the reasons why so few people are to be found who seem sensible and pleasant in conversation is that almost everybody is thinking about what he wants to say himself, rather than about answering clearly what is said to him.

The more clever and polite think it enough simply to put on an attentive expression, while all the while you can see in their eyes and train of thought that they are far removed from what you are saying and are anxious to get back to what they want to say. They ought, on the contrary, to reflect that such keenness to please oneself is a bad way of pleasing or persuading others and that to listen well and answer to the point is one of the most perfect qualities one can have in conversation.

Francois La Rochefoucauld

◆

It has been written that life is divided into three terms: that which was, that which is, and that which will be. Let us learn from the past to profit by the present, and from the present to live better for the future.

◆

A CAPSULE COURSE IN HUMAN RELATIONS

1. The five most important words are these:
   "I am proud of you."
2. The four most important words are these:
   "What is your opinion?"
3. The three most important words are these:
   "If you please."
4. The two most important words are these:
   "Thank you."
5. The least important word is:
   "I"

Robert Woodruff

True humility is not an abject, groveling, self-despising spirit; it is but a right estimate of ourselves as God sees us.

Tryon Edwards

I gather flowers by the wayside, by the brooks and in the meadows. And only the string with which I bind them together is my own.

Michel Eyquem de Montaigne

A Roman poet said: "Let ancient times delight other folk; I rejoice that I was not born till now."

When you deal in generalities, you will never have a success. When you deal in specifics, you will rarely have a failure.

Thomas S. Monson

Life and Learning

Princes come, princes go; an hour of pomp and show they know.

Robert Craig Wright

"Father, where shall I work today?"
And my love flowed warm and free.
Then He pointed me out a tiny spot
And said, "Tend that for me."

I answered quickly, "Oh, no, not that,
Why no one would ever see
No matter how well my work was done;
Not that little place for me."

And the word He spoke, it was not stern;
He answered me tenderly:
"Ah, little one, search that heart of thine;
Art thou working for them or me?
Nazareth was a little place,
And so was Galilee."

Meade MacGuire

Thou that hast given so much to me, give one thing more: a grateful heart.

George Herbert

There is a tendency among men to kiss the foot above and kick the head below on the ladder of life.

John A. Widtsoe

We are preoccupied with material things. Our supreme god is technology; our goddess is sex. Most of us are more interested in getting to the moon than in getting to heaven, more concerned about conquering space than about conquering ourselves. We are more dedicated to material security than to inner purity. We give much more thought to what we wear, what we eat, what we drink and what we can do to relax than we give to what we are.

Billy Graham

I believe we are living in one of the most precious and privileged periods of all human history — a period of change and challenge and infinite promise.

The criteria of emotional maturity consists of:

1. Having the ability to deal constructively with reality.
2. Having the capacity to change.
3. Having a relative freedom from symptoms that are produced by tensions and anxieties.
4. Having the capacity to find more satisfaction in giving than receiving.
5. Having the capacity to relate to other people in a consistent manner, with mutual satisfaction and helpfulness.
6. Having the capacity to sublimate, to direct one's instinctive hostile energy into creative and constructive outlets.
7. Having the capacity to love.

Dr. William C. Menninger

MY WAGE

I bargained with Life for a penny,
And Life would pay no more,
However I begged at evening
When I counted my scanty store;

For Life is a just employer,
He gives you what you ask,
But once you have set the wages,
Why, you must bear the task.

I worked for a menial's hire,
Only to learn, dismayed,
That any wage I had asked of Life,
Life would have paid.

Jessie B. Rittenhouse

To strive, to seek, to find, and not to yield.

Alfred, Lord Tennyson

Those who forget the past will tend to repeat it, with all its attendant sorrows.

Dr. William F. Adams

What was most significant about the lunar voyage was not that men set foot on the moon but that they set eye on the earth.

Norman Cousins

Take things with gratitude, rather than for granted.

James Reston

In a civil defense test, during a mock air raid, Boy Scouts were to impersonate wounded people who would be picked up by the defense units. One Scout, after lying "wounded" for several hours, evidently got a little disgusted; the squad that came to "rescue" him found his scrawled note: "Have bled to death and gone home."

There's nothing wrong in change if it is in the right direction.

Sir Winston Churchill

Nothing is permanent in life except change.

Chinese Proverb

Life is God's gift to man. What we do with our life is our gift to God.

Harold B. Lee

This time, like all times, is a very good one, if we but know what to do with it. I ask not for the great, the remote, the romantic. Give me insight into today, and you may have the antique and future worlds.

Ralph Waldo Emerson

Life and Learning

LIFE

Life is a gift to be used every day,
Not to be smothered and hidden away;
It isn't a thing to be stored in the chest
Where you gather your keepsakes and treasure your best;
It isn't a joy to be sipped now and then,
And promptly put back in a dark place again.

Life is a gift that the humblest may boast of,
And one that the humblest may well make the most of;
Get out and live it each hour of the day,
Wear it and use it as much as you may;
Don't keep it in niches and corners and grooves —
You'll find that in service its beauty improves.

Edgar A. Guest

Life by the yard is hard; by the inch it's a cinch.

Quality in living is not a newly sought way of life. Several thousand years ago the sacred book of Egypt pictured moral perfection. The soul pleading before Osiris and the celestial jury said: "I have told no lies, committed no frauds, promoted no strife, caused no one to weep, made no fraudulent gains; I have sown joy and not sorrow, given food to the hungry and clothed the naked."

Quality living does not consist merely in not doing wrong. There are people in every age who stand out head and shoulders above others. They are people who have something to do and who do it well.

Royal Bank of Canada Newsletter

God gave us memories, that in life's garden we may have June roses in December.

John Barrie

The memory strengthens as you lay burdens upon it and becomes trustworthy as you trust it.

Thomas De Quincey

I do not believe the greatest threat to our future is from bombs or guided missiles. I don't think our civilization will die that way. I think it will die when we no longer care. Arnold Toynbee has pointed out that nineteen or twenty-one civilizations have died from within and not by conquest from without. There were no bands playing and flags waving when these civilizations decayed. It happened slowly, in the quiet and the dark when no one was aware.

Laurence M. Gould

Our responsibility is to be program-oriented but people-centered. We labor with our hands, with our heads, with our hearts.

To lack wisdom is no disgrace. To lack the desire for wisdom is a pity. But to desire wisdom and not know how to find it is a tragedy.

Leon Gutterman

Life and Learning

◆

Change is part of a law of life. We must grow physically from childhood to adulthood, mentally from ignorance to knowledge, emotionally from insecurity to stability and spiritually to an abiding faith in a living God.

◆

In Shakespeare's *Henry VIII*, Cardinal Wolsey bemoans his fate: "Had I but served my God with half the zeal with which I served my king, He would not in mine age have left me naked to mine enemies."

The sweetness of success had turned into the bitter wormwood of disappointment and defeat. Wolsey commanded tremendous power and prestige, second only to the king. History records that he was arrogant, imperious and extravagant and that people kowtowed to him out of fear. He was spoiled by obeisance and flattery.

Then came the fatal blow. Charged with high treason by Henry VIII, his false friends removed their masks and revealed their real feelings. He became a sick old man, disappointed and brokenhearted. Then he realized the limitations of power and the sin of abusing and misusing it. When it was all too late, he understood the wisdom of Ecclesiastes: "Vanity of vanities, all is vanity."

Rabbi Magnin

◆

This is the triumph of man:

Where there is truth, he must find.
Where there is destruction, he must rebuild.
Where there is love, he must protect.

World's Fair Exhibit

◆

Man is born abroad and spends his life searching for his
home.

Charlie Freed

There is a tide in the affairs of men,
Which, taken at the flood, leads on to fortune;
Omitted, all the voyage of their life
Is bound in shallows and in miseries.
On such a full sea are we now afloat,
We must take the current when it serves,
Or lose our ventures.

William Shakespeare

The true secret of life is to live outside of oneself in
love.

It was the best of times, it was the worst of times; it was
the age of wisdom, it was the age of foolishness; it was the
epoch of belief, it was the epoch of incredulity; it was the
season of Light, it was the season of Darkness; it was the
spring of hope, it was the winter of despair. We had
everything before us, we had nothing before us.

Charles Dickens

Give without remembering; receive without forgetting.

Diane Barton

Life and Learning

Of all sad words of tongue or pen,
The saddest are these: "It might have been."

James Greenleaf Whittier

Disappointment is never so bitter, so "sour grapes," as when one has had superior advantages and has neglected them or frittered them away or watered them down.

Sign seen in front of a Protestant church in Melbourne, Australia: Before Easter there must be a cross.

On a motion to award the great general Napoleon a pension, the French Assembly decided that "such glorious deeds could not be rewarded by gold," so they gave him nothing.

What some motorists should keep in mind is that it's not only the automobile that can be recalled by its maker.

We cannot go to heaven in a feather bed. The Savior of the world entered after great pain and suffering. We, as servants, can expect no more than the Master.

Do not forget the hands of the aged; they have touched much of life and have become sensitive and sympathetic.

You can't do today's work on yesterday's equipment if you expect to be in business tomorrow.

When youth is gone, every man will look back upon that period of his life with infinite sorrow and regret. It is the bitter sorrow and regret of a man who knows that once he had a great talent and wasted it; once he had a great treasure and got nothing from it. It is the sorrow of one who knows that he had strength enough for everything and never used it.

Thomas Wolfe

God's wonders are many, but man is the greatest wonder of all.

Alexander the Great

Cicero mentions the following six mistakes of man:

1. The delusion that individual advancement is made by crushing others.
2. The tendency to worry about things that cannot be corrected.
3. Insisting that a thing is impossible because we cannot accomplish it.
4. Refusing to set aside trivial preferences.
5. Neglecting development and refinement of the mind and not acquiring the habit of reading and studying.
6. Attempting to compel other persons to believe and live as we do.

Life and Learning

To the past, to the present, and the future I dedicate this book. To the past because I came out of it. To the present because I live in it. To the future because my children will inherit it.

Ruth May Fox

MY CREED

I will be dependable.
I will make prayerful preparation.
I will make this duty a pleasure.
I will leave my troubles at home.
I will bring sunshine into the homes I visit.
I will speak well of everyone.
I will not gossip.
I will not betray a confidence.
I will seek to know the needs of the people I visit.
I will attend my meetings.
I will live worthy of this calling.

When provided with sound economic education, citizens will no longer be deceived by catch phrases, demagogic outbursts, mild impeachments or glowing reassurances, all intended to frighten or appease.

They will then become adult economic realists. They will not be misled, terrorized or won over to new-sounding philosophies and creeds which, in the face of all experience, stand utterly condemned and branded as the cause of the collapse of nations and civilizations.

Orval W. Adams

———————◆———————

Wise men talk because they have something to say, fools because they have to say something.

Plato

———————◆———————

The history of mankind is strewn with habits and creeds and dogmas that were essential in one age and disastrous in another.

James Reston

———————◆———————

Nothing, good or bad, remains static. Change is the normal state in the world today, and a person needs to be resourceful in altering his plans to meet new circumstances.

Royal Bank of Canada Newsletter

———————◆———————

Nothing is constant but change.

Edward Atkinson

———————◆———————

From an article entitled "Uruguay: Utopia Gone Wild," which appeared in the May 1966 issue of *Reader's Digest:* Labor wanted higher wages; industrialists wanted bigger income; but nobody wanted to do any work. Citizens thought more of their rights than of their obligations. The country's vast web of social legislation redistributed wealth but did not create it. Nobody had the vision to see that what Uruguay needed was production. Said President Washington Beltran: "We are in a state of crisis—one created solely by our own institutions."

———————◆———————

258

Life and Learning

An institution is the lengthened shadow of one man. All history resolves itself very easily into the biography of a few stout and earnest persons.

Ralph Waldo Emerson

Signs by which maturity may be tested:
1. Live the Golden Rule.
2. Find your talent and develop it.
3. Keep on learning.

Dr. Harry Allen Overstreet

A ruler devised a test to see which of the people in his kingdom were sane. The sane ones could continue to live in the kingdom; the others could not. He had built a building which had in it a tank into which flowed a stream of water from a pipe in the wall. Each person would be given a bucket of water and told to empty the tank. If he stopped the flow first and then emptied the tank, he was judged sane.

It is a far, far better thing that I do, than I have ever done; it is a far, far better rest that I go to, than I have ever known.

Charles Dickens

A life spent in digging is worth nothing if you plant no olive trees.

Sicilian Proverb

---◆---

All men are born equal, but they seem to be born equal to different things — and that's the difference.

---◆---

When we pick up our newspaper at breakfast, we expect — we even demand — that it bring us momentous events since the night before. We turn on the car radio as we drive to work and expect "news" to have occurred since the morning newspaper went to press.

Returning in the evening, we expect our house not only to shelter us, to keep us warm in winter and cool in summer, but also to relax us, to dignify us, to encompass us with soft music and interesting hobbies, to be a playground, a theater. We expect our two-week vacation to be romantic, exotic, cheap, and effortless. We expect a far-away atmosphere if we go to a nearby place; and we expect everything to be relaxing, sanitary, and Americanized if we go to a far-away place. We expect new heroes every season, a literary masterpiece every month, a dramatic spectacular every week, a rare sensation every night. We expect everybody to feel free to disagree, yet we expect everybody to be loyal, not to rock the boat or take the Fifth Amendment.

We expect everybody to believe deeply in his religion, yet not to think less of others for not believing. We expect our nation to be strong and great and vast and varied and prepared for every challenge; yet we expect our "national purpose" to be clear and simple, something that gives direction to the lives of two hundred million people and yet can be bought in a paperback at the corner drugstore for a dollar.

We expect anything and everything. We expect the contradictory and the impossible. We expect compact cars

---◆---

---◆---

which are spacious, luxurious cars which are economical. We expect to be rich and charitable, powerful and merciful, active and reflective, kind and competitive. We expect to be inspired by mediocre appeals for "excellence," to be made literate by illiterate appeals for literacy. We expect to eat and stay thin, to be constantly on the move and ever more neighborly.

Daniel J. Boorstin

---◆---

History is a vast early-warning system.

Norman Cousins

---◆---

MONEY

Workers earn it,
Spendthrifts burn it,
Bankers lend it,
Women spend it,
Forgers fake it,
Taxes take it,
Dying leave it,
Heirs receive it,
Thrifty save it,
Misers crave it,
Robbers seize it,
Rich increase it,
Gamblers lose it,
I could use it.

Richard Armour

---◆---

---◆---

If you have ever leaned on a farm fence at twilight and heard the spring peepers peep, if you have ever stopped while crossing a pasture to listen for a bobwhite, if you have ever breathed fresh air on a high hill or picked watercress by a cool spring or felt the warmth in the cow barn on a January morning, then you are a farmer in spirit as long as you live.

John T. Cunningham

---◆---

The word *economics,* traced to its Greek root, means "the laws of the house."

---◆---

Economic illiteracy is a serious problem. The terrible fact is that a citizen may acquire a high school diploma without once having been exposed to basic economics. He may have passed everything from geometry to Greek mythology and still know next to nothing about the bread and butter system by which he lives.

---◆---

A nation becomes what its young people read in their youth. Its ideals are fashioned then. Its goals are strongly determined. And the foundations are established for future action.

James A. Michener

---◆---

Inscription on the wall of the Library of Congress: "Science is organized knowledge."

---◆---

Life and Learning

―――――――――――◆―――――――――――

Anyone may put off decision-making by the simple device of donning a mask under cover of which he analyzes and re-analyzes a problem, postponing the moment he fears.

Royal Bank of Canada Newsletter

―――――――――――◆―――――――――――

Sometimes the statement that a man has no time to read sounds like a boast. Its maker means to say that he is too important, too occupied with big affairs to fritter away time in reading. But reading is a legitimate business activity, designed to provide the mental food which maintains the intellectual life so greatly needed in business.

Reading is one of the true pleasures of life. In our age of mass culture, when so much that we encounter is abridged, adapted, adulterated, shredded and boiled down, and commercialism's loud speakers are incessantly braying, it is mind-easing and mind-inspiring to sit down privately with a congenial book.

Royal Bank of Canada Newsletter

―――――――――――◆―――――――――――

A principle is not like a rule. The rule asks nothing more of you than that you obey; a principle requires you to do your own thinking. A rule gives you credit only for being a creature; a principle gives you stature.

―――――――――――◆―――――――――――

It is well for a man to respect his own vocation — whatever it is — and to think himself bound to uphold it and claim for it the respect it deserves.

Charles Dickens

―――――――――――◆―――――――――――

If a man is satisfied with his work, he is likely to live longer. A study at Duke University showed that job satisfaction is necessary for general happiness, and that happiness promotes good health and probably long life.

Prevention

Newton was loafing under an apple tree when he saw an apple fall and got the gravitation idea; James Watt was loafing in the kitchen when the kettle boiled and he got the idea of the steam engine; Galileo was letting his mind wander from the sermon while he watched the lamp swinging in the cathedral at Pisa and developed the pendulum principle.

The person who travels with his mind relaxed from the narrow circle of his daily pursuits is well on the way to thinking up new ideas and developing ideas that have been buried in his mind under the load of daily work.

Winifred A. Peterson

To be ignorant is not a crime; but to abide in ignorance when it can be avoided — that is a crime against oneself.

It is reputed that an interviewer talked once to the wife of Albert Einstein and asked her, "What do you know about the theory of relativity?"

She replied, "I know nothing about the theory of relativity, but I know everything about Albert Einstein, and that is more than he knows."

Life and Learning

———————◆———————

Perhaps some of the philosophy that made John Wayne what he was came from his pharmacist father, Clyde Morrison, who had three rules he passed on to his sons: (1) Always keep your word; (2) A gentleman never insults anyone intentionally; (3) Don't look for trouble, but if you get into a fight, make sure you win it!

Deseret News Editorial
Salt Lake City, Utah

———————◆———————

Wrath is cruel, and anger is outrageous; but who is able to stand before jealousy?

———————◆———————

Reading stretches our mental muscles and expands our horizons. It takes us out of our mundane worlds and lets us travel as far as our imaginations and the picture painting words of the authors can carry us. Reading keeps us vibrant; it keeps us alive and makes us far more interesting to our marriage mates and our families. It also is a form of insurance against mental aging. We are only as old as we think we are. Some people say that one way to keep alive is to keep interested in many things, and the way to keep interested is to read widely.

Royal Bank of Canada Newsletter

———————◆———————

Education of the heart is the heart of education.

Hugh B. Brown

———————◆———————

In your thinking, substitute *something* for *something*, rather than *something* for *nothing*.

———————◆———————

Knowledge is gained one truth at a time.

He who knows not and knows not that he knows not
Is a fool — shun him.
He who knows not and knows that he knows not
Is simple — teach him.
He who knows and knows not that he knows
Is asleep — awaken him.
He who knows and knows that he knows
Is wise — follow him.

Unknown

A person learns more rapidly from what he does than from what others do for him. One expert has concluded that "the ratio of learning is: one by hearing, ten by seeing, and one thousand by doing." A person does not learn nearly so well by sitting and listening to someone talk as he does by participating. He must be involved in the lesson. The secret of successful teaching, therefore, is getting a person to do something for himself. A class in physical education would not get much physical exercise if the teacher, day after day, went through the exercises herself and left the class idle. Someone else's tongue wagging is not enough activity to keep students alert. The scriptures also stress the importance of activity: "Be ye doers of the word, and not hearers only." (James 1:22.)

There are enough unfulfilled tasks to keep everybody busy.

When you ignore, you injure. When you inform, you inspire.

Thomas S. Monson

To insure the education of their teenagers, parents need to pull a few wires: television, telephone and ignition!

These Times

A jewelry store owner in Ohio has had two diamonds — $700 each — set in his front teeth. He comments: "They look like two headlights. Basically, all men are alike. I wanted to be different."

We are not born equal; we are born unique. Finding our strengths, our unique powers should be the purpose of the journey of life.

Earl Nightingale

The great Canadian physician Sir William Osler worked out a psychological plan for concentrating action into what he termed "daytight compartments," like the watertight compartments of ships. "Each of you is bound on a long voyage," he once told a group of students at Yale University. "By touching a button at every level of your life you can close the iron doors shutting out the past — the dear yesterdays. Touch another and shut out the future — the unborn tomorrows. Then you are safe — safe for today."

Royal Bank of Canada Newsletter

In education, the "newest" does not necessarily make for the "best" education. To my limited knowledge, nothing as effective has yet been invented for transmission of knowledge from one mind to another as the so-called Socratic method. According to Western tradition, the two greatest teachers were Socrates and Jesus Christ. Both individualized their teaching. The Socratic technique was to bring the learner to recognition of a concept or generalization through teacher-led discussion. Christ communicated in a forceful and lucid way with individuals and with groups of individuals.

James K. Wellington

IN FLANDERS FIELDS

In Flanders fields the poppies blow
Between the crosses, row on row,
That mark our place; and in the sky
The larks, still bravely singing, fly
Scarce heard amid the guns below.

We are the Dead. Short days ago
We lived, felt dawn, saw sunset glow,
Loved and were loved, and now we lie
In Flanders fields.

Take up our quarrel with the foe:
To you from failing hands we throw
The torch; be yours to hold it high.
If ye break faith with us who die
We shall not sleep, though poppies grow
In Flanders fields.

John McCrae

268

Life and Learning

An educated man stands, as it were, in the midst of a boundless arsenal and magazine, filled with all the weapons and engines which man's skill has been able to devise from the earliest time; and he works, accordingly, with a strength borrowed from all past ages. How different is *his* state who stands on the outside of that storehouse and feels that its gates must be stormed or remain forever shut against him! His means are the commonest and rudest; the mere work done is no measure of his strength. A dwarf behind his steam engine may remove mountains; but no dwarf will hew them down with a pick axe, and he must be a Titan that hurls them abroad with his arms.

Thomas Carlyle

We know that television and computers are having a profound impact on our society and the world. At one time there were three major socializing influences: family, church and school. Now there is a fourth: television, with computer technology not far behind.

The economic and sociological implications for America are staggering — but we know appallingly little about them. For example, we know we must have a new generation of well-educated children to deal with this information society — but quite the reverse is occurring. For the first time in our history, the generation graduating from school is less literate than its parents. We don't know why, but we cannot shrug it off. Our nation will not remain strong if a large portion of the population is excluded from meaningful economic, political, or social participation because it cannot comprehend or deal with the demands of this new age.

Timothy E. Wirth

Your first duty in life is towards your afterself. So live that your afterself — the man you ought to be — may in his time be possible and actual.

Far away in the years he is waiting his turn. His body, his brain, his soul, are in your boyish hands. He cannot help himself. What will you leave for him? Will it be a brain unspoiled by lust or dissipation; a mind trained to think and act; a nervous system as true as a dial in its response to the truth about you? Will you let him come as a man among men in his time? Or will you throw away his inheritance before he has had the chance to touch it?

Will you turn over to him a brain distorted; a mind diseased; a will untrained to action; a spinal cord grown through and through with the devil grass we call wild oats? Will you let him come taking your place, gaining through your experiences, happy in your friendships, hallowed through your joys, building them on his own?

Or will you fling it all away, decreeing, wantonlike, that the man you might have been shall never be?

This is your problem in life — the problem vastly more important to you than any or all others. How will you meet it — as a man or as a fool? It is your problem today and every day, and the hour of your decision is the crisis in your destiny.

David Starr Jordan

Time is precious, but life is priceless.

Whatever I did not know, I was not ashamed to inquire about; so I acquired knowledge.

Life and Learning

CHILDREN'S LETTERS TO GOD

"Dear God: I wished on a star two times but nothing happened. Now what? Anna."

"Dear God: If you made the rule for kids to take out the garbage, please change it. Maurice."

"Dear Holy God: Would you make it so there would not be any more wars? And so every one could vote. Also everybody should have a lot of fun. Nancy."

"Dear God: Charles, my cat, got run over. And if you made it happen, you have to tell me why. Harvey."

"Dear God: I read your book and I like it. I would like to write a book some day with the same kind of stories. Where do you get your ideas? Best wishes, Mark."

Time

There are nine requisites for contented living:

1. Health enough to make work a pleasure.
2. Wealth enough to support your needs.
3. Strength enough to battle with difficulties and forsake them.
4. Grace enough to confess your sins and overcome them.
5. Patience enough to toil until some good is accomplished.
6. Charity enough to see some good in your neighbor.
7. Love enough to move you to be useful and helpful to others.
8. Faith enough to make real the things of God.
9. Hope enough to remove all anxious fears concerning the future.

Johann Wolfgang von Goethe

DESIDERATA

Go placidly amid the noise and the haste, and remember what peace there may be in silence. As far as possible, without surrender, be on good terms with all persons. Speak your truth quietly and clearly; and listen to others, even to the dull and the ignorant; they, too, have their story. Avoid loud and aggressive persons. They are vexations to the spirit. If you compare yourself with others, you may become vain or bitter, for always there will be greater and lesser persons than yourself.

Enjoy your achievements as well as your plans. Keep interested in your own career, however humble; it is a real possession in the changing fortunes of time. Exercise caution in your business affairs, for the world is full of trickery, but let not this blind you to what virtue there is; many persons strive for high ideals, and everywhere life is full of heroism.

Be yourself. Especially do not feign affection, neither be cynical about love; for in the face of all aridity and disenchantment, it is as perennial as the grass.

Take kindly the counsel of the years, gracefully surrendering the things of youth. Nurture strength of spirit to shield you in sudden misfortune. But do not distress yourself with dark imaginings: many fears are born of fatigue and loneliness.

Beyond a wholesome discipline, be gentle with yourself. You are a child of the universe no less than the trees and the stars; you have a right to be here. And whether or not it is clear to you, no doubt the universe is unfolding as it should. Therefore be at peace with God, whatever you conceive Him to be. And whatever your labors and

---

aspirations, in the noisy confusion of life, keep peace in your soul. With all its sham, drudgery, and broken dreams, it is still a beautiful world. Be cheerful. Strive to be happy.

Max Ehrmann

"You can be a baseball player and get an education, too," my father told me. We had an old car that was parked in our yard, and we sat in that car and talked and talked. I told him I was going to drop out of school when I got a chance to play baseball. He turned around and put his hand on my shoulder.

"Son, I quit school because I had to go to work to make a living. You don't have to. I put fifty cents on that dresser each morning for you to take to school to buy your lunch and whatever else you need. I only take twenty-five cents to work with me. It's worth more to me that you get an education than it is for me to eat. So let's hear no more about dropping out of school."

You don't forget this kind of sacrifice by your father. Herbert Aaron was always ready to deny himself something if it would help his family.

Henry "Hank" Aaron

There's an old Arabian proverb that goes: A fool may be known by six things: anger without cause; speech without profit; change without progress; inquiry without object; putting trust in a stranger; and mistaking foes for friends.

Earl Nightingale

A PSALM OF LIFE

Tell me not, in mournful numbers,
Life is but an empty dream!—
For the soul is dead that slumbers,
And things are not what they seem.

Life is real! Life is earnest!
And the grave is not its goal;
Dust thou art, to dust returnest,
Was not spoken of the soul.

Not enjoyment, and not sorrow,
If our destined end or way;
But to act, that each tomorrow
Find us farther than today.

Art is long, and Time is fleeting,
And our hearts, though stout and brave,
Still, like muffled drums, are beating
Funeral marches to the grave.

In the world's broad field of battle,
In the bivouac of life,
Be not like dumb, driven cattle!
Be a hero in the strife!

Trust no Future, howe'er pleasant!
Let the dead Past bury its dead!
Act,—act in the living Present!
Heart within, and God o'erhead!

Lives of great men all remind us
We can make our lives sublime,
And, departing, leave behind us
Footprints on the sands of time.

Footprints, that perhaps another,
Sailing o'er life's solemn main,

A forlorn and shipwrecked brother,
Seeing, shall take heart again.

Let us then be up and doing,
With a heart for any fate;
Still achieving, still pursuing,
Learn to labor and to wait.

Henry Wadsworth Longfellow

So live that when thy summons comes to join the innumerable caravan that moves to that mysterious realm where each shall take his chamber in the silent halls of death, thou go not like the quarry-slave at night, scourged to his dungeon; but, sustained and soothed by an unfaltering trust, approach thy grave like one who wraps the drapery of his couch about him and lies down to pleasant dreams.

William Cullen Bryant

O, DRY THOSE TEARS

O, dry those tears and calm those fears;
Life is not made for sorrow.
'Twill come, alas! but soon 'twill pass;
Clouds will be sunshine tomorrow.

O, lift thine eyes to the blue skies;
See how the clouds do borrow
Sunshine each one, straight from the sun;
So is it ever with sorrow.

Then lift thine eyes to the blue skies,
Clouds will be sunshine tomorrow.
O, dry those tears and calm those fears;
Life is not made for sorrow.

Life and Learning

◆

The only responsibility that a man cannot evade in this life is the one he thinks of least—his personal influence. A man's conscious influence is woefully small. But his unconscious influence—the silent, subtle radiations of his personality, the effect of his words and acts, the trifles he never considers—is tremendous. Every man has an atmosphere which is affecting every other. So silent and unconsciously is this influence working that many men forget that it exists. Into the hand of every man is given marvelous power for good or for evil—the silent, unconscious, unseen influence of his life. This is simply the constant radiation of what a man is—not what he pretends to be. Every man, by his mere living, can radiate sympathy, happiness, hope, or any of a hundred qualities. There are men whose presence seems to radiate sunshine, cheer, optimism. With them you feel calm and rested and restored, in a moment, to a new and stronger faith in humanity.

William George Jordan

◆

Index of Authors

277

Index of Authors

Index of Authors

Index of Titles

Index of Titles

◆

Index of Titles

281

Index of First Lines

◆

282

Index of First Lines

Index of First Lines

285

Index of First Lines

Index of First Lines

Index of First Lines

Index of First Lines

Index of First Lines

Index of First Lines

Index of First Lines

Index of First Lines

295

Index of First Lines